Coming To The Mercy Seat

J.e Franklin's

Ten-Minute Folk Dramas

The First Decatet

Published By
Blackgirl Ensemble Theatre, Inc
Designed by
SunRASon *Production Company*

Visit us online at
www.sunrason.com

Published by
Blackgirl Ensemble Theatre, Inc
P.O. 517
NY, NY 10031
Email: JE413@AOL.COM
www.geocities.com/haveplaywilltravel/playseries.html

Consultation & Design By
SunRASon **Prod, Co.**
P.O. Box 2020
Canal St. Station
NY, NY 10013
Ph: (718) 444-7464
WWW.SUNRASON.COM
Email: info@sunrason.com

Copyright (C) 2003 by J. E. Franklin
Design and layout by Tehut-Nine & Heru Ptah
Cover Design by Tehut-Nine
Cover Concept by J.E. Franklin

No part of this book may be reproduced or utilized in any form or by any means, electronic or mechanical, including photocopying, recording, or by any information storage or retrieval system, without permission from the author.

Inquiries should be addressed to:

Blackgirl Ensemble Theater, Inc.
P. O. Box 517
New York, NY 10031

Special limited edition
Printed in the United States of America

ISBN: 0-97 46669-0-4

WHAT THE CRITICS ARE SAYING:

"Drawn on the African-American church experience...but reaches out and becomes universal...very powerful."
    Barbara Lounsberry,
    Waterloo Courier

"An Impressive experience of a religious quality."
    Edward Amend,
    KHKE

"Exceedingly sophisticated drama and emotional sensitivity."
    KUNI Public Radio

"Franklin gets at the core of the bottled-up rage that prompts us to strike out."
    Herb Boyd
    The Black World Today

"Franklin mixes humor with brutal reality! One of the few playwrights of her stature working in the Ten-Minute genre."
    Yusef Salaam
    The Amsterdam News

TABLE OF CONTENTS

Poetic Intro	5
Acknowledgments	7
Dedication	8
Preface	9
Introduction	12
A Director's Notes	19
Poetic Intro	24
Hot Methuselah	25
Poetic Intro	44
The Closer The Kin	45
Poetic Intro	60
Left Shoe's Buddy	61
Poetic Intro	75
Puttin' Mama In The Ground	76
Poetic Intro	90
Spanky's Pop	91
Poetic Intro	108
Two Mens'es Daughter	109
Poetic Intro	125
Shacking Up Grey	126
Poetic Intro	138
Puttin' Pippy Away	139
Poetic Intro	152
S'pozed-To-Be Daddy	153
Poetic Intro	165
Solomon's Way	166
Photos	180
Other Works By The Author	184
Biographical Information	185

Coming to The Mercy Seat

Am I bound to the full-length?
Stuffed to capacity with lines
And monologues of characters
And plots I don't understand,
Don't appreciate, and plain don't like?

Usually...

I'm interested in the beginning
Lulled to sleep towards the middle,
And awakened by thunderous applause
At the end of 2 1/2 hours of...
"What were they trying to say?"

Can I get something short and sweet?
You know, to the point.
Make me laugh, make me cry.
Let me discuss with my theater buddy
Which Ten-minute plays we liked best.

Ms. Goldie had me cracking up,
And the story with the two old sisters
Had me wishing I had a sister.

Switch it up for me.
Give me variety.
Define a play.
Give me the Ten-Minute play.

N'zinga

Nzinga is an actress and spoken word artist who has performed at theatres and other venues around the country, including the St. James Theatre, The Nuyorican Poets Café, The Louis Abrons Arts Center and Applause Theatre Bookstore. She is a graduate of Morgan State University, where she studied music under Dr. Nathan Carter.

Her poetry introduces each play.

A special thanks to Dr. Scharron Clayton, Dr. Jerry Komia Domatob, Tehut-Nine and to my daughter, N'zinga Franklin, for their help and encouragement.

For my sister, Rosemary Franklin Wilson
For my brother, Rev. Benjamin Franklin
And for Thomas Firrell Franklin...wherever you are.

Preface

J. E. Franklin's Dramatic Excellence and Versatility

J. E. Franklin, a talented writer, commentator, sociologist and dramatist, sparks debates, commentary, laughter and reflections in her plays. Blending political insight, economic analysis and philosophical observations, J. E. tackles historical and contemporary issues that affect humans globally.

THEMES

Bold and courageous, J. E. Franklin focuses on themes such as: African-American identity, class struggles, poverty, disease, unemployment, etc. She daringly spotlights hot topics, notably racism, AIDS, teenage pregnancy, juvenile delinquency, crime, political intrigues and economic disparity in America and elsewhere with remarkable wit, frankness and dexterity. She exposes problems, raises philosophical questions and proposes practical solutions.

HUMOR

Although J. E. addresses serious themes, humor graces her plays. She infuses comic relief, laughter and occasional light-heartedness in the dramas. Certain scenes evoke the best in comedy. Perhaps she should direct her formidable talents towards the movie and television industries.

LANGUAGE

In clear, lucid and vivid language, J. E. communicates with simplicity. Her characters' speeches tie logically with the discourse. She uses jargon, slogans, vernacular and professional language when appropriate. One of J. E. Franklin's major strengths is her mastery of the English language and her outstanding skills in adapting dialects to suit protagonists and minor characters.

The language thus matches characters, who are largely symbols for major social causes. The characters' voices, tones, pitches and styles affirm story lines. Her emphasis on ideas places her in the formidable league of the famous British writer, George Bernard Shaw, who was a leading dramatic and social ideologue of the 19th century.

EXCELLENCE

Additionally, J. E. uses soliloquies and ventriloquists. Characters embark on public monologues as Shakespearean creations who meditate aloud on triumphs and tragedies. Her unique blend and juxtaposition of good and bad, heroism and villainy, tragedy and comedy is phenomenal. The contrast and balance is splendid.

DIALOGUE

However, J. E. Franklin excels with dialogue. When you listen to the characters or watch them on stage, they sound as human beings. The discussions are authentic, and that enhances verisimilitude.

REALISM & REFORM

J. E. Franklin's realism is manifested in her down-to-earth themes that disavow the idealism, which obscures plays. The language is direct, sometimes journalistic and vivid. She comes across as a militant crusader, championing reform and even revolution. J. E. does not languish in the skies dabbling in dreams, fancy and fantasy.

She communicates with people, addressing daily problems, provoking thought, educating, alerting, alarming, instructing, interpreting and entertaining.

J. E. Franklin is one of the foremost social commentators, critics and dramatists of our time. Please read and enjoy. Introduce the plays to others and promote them for posterity. Let us congratulate and salute J. E. Franklin, an excellent writer, a versatile artist and a literary giant.

Dr. Jerry Komia Domatob
Department of Communications
Rutgers University

*Dr. Jerry Komia Domatob has published in several journals internationally. He is the author of the books African-Americans of Eastern Long Island; African-Americans of Western Long Island; and African-Americans of Waterloo. He currently teaches at Rutgers **University.***

INTRODUCTION

I've gone through several phases in my writing career, and 1989 began what I call my elder-character phase. Although before 1989, I had certainly written elder characters into my work, the elder had never been at the center. A combination of factors changed all this. One of those factors was my almost yearly visit to my uncle's home in Texas. But the factor which had the greatest influence on my decision to write my first Ten-Minute play was something I witnessed at a rehearsal of one of my plays.

I can't remember which one of my full-length plays was in rehearsal, but I'll never forget the scene I saw when I walked in the door. Pages of my script were scattered about the stage floor, and other pages were floating and flipping, on their way to the floor. The script had come unbound, and the actor—somewhere in her seventies—was struggling to find the pages and put them back in order. Even with both her hands, she didn't have the dexterity to re-order everything. As I watched the rehearsal, I also saw her struggling to learn her lines and remember her cues.
  I thought about this and about what I had observed of my uncle's declining abilities, and some months later, I determined to write a shorter work, one the actors could at least hold in their hands. And so I did.

The first Ten-Minute play I wrote was "Hot Methuselah," a comedy about an elder who threatens to end her forty-year marriage to her husband when she catches him romancing a girl young enough to be his great granddaughter. After I wrote the play, I set it aside, the way I do everything I finish, waiting for the day when someone might show some interest in it. Then one day, in the Dramatist Guild Quarterly, I saw a reminder of an approaching deadline for the Ten-Minute play contest at Actors Theater of Louisville. I entered "Hot Methuselah."

Around the same time, I received a call about a visiting professorship in the theater department at the University of Iowa's MFA program. I submitted *Hot Methuselah* as a sample of my writing, got the position immediately and saw my appointment as a chance to introduce my students to the Ten-Minute genre. The form had challenged me, and I believed it would challenge other writers. I found it to be an excellent teaching tool.

After I heard a first reading of *Hot Methuselah* by a group of student actors from the University's Playwrights Lab, I thought the work had failed. Tisch Jones, a directing student in my Script Analysis class, had directed the reading. Although some of the lines had worked for me, the reading had dampened my spirit, and I had no intention of pursuing the genre. It was only a reading, and I might have factored in a few things: the youth and inexperience of the actors, their unfamiliarity with the genre, and their brief rehearsal time. Instead, I blamed the tepid reception the work received on something amiss in the script.

This sense was reinforced in the weeks that followed by the rejection of the play by Actors Theater of Louisville. I had put a lot of stock in Louisville's ruling...too much, in fact; years later, in retrospect, I realized I shouldn't have. Putting too much stock in a theater's opinion of a work is a mistake many playwrights make. Initially, though, I thought it was the work. After all, the genre was new to me. I asked myself, "Should the play have been a ten page monologue? Would it then have qualified as a Ten-Minute play?"

According to my sense of the problem, the work had conformed in every way to the technical definition of a Ten-Minute play, i. e., *a work for the stage which does not exceed ten typewritten pages*. At the time, I hadn't yet read or seen a Ten-Minute play staged or performed. Inspiration and instinct alone had been my guiding principles. Since that first rejection of *Hot Methuselah* by the Actor's Theater of Louisville, I've understood that a theater rejects a play for a number of reasons, many of which have little or nothing to do with lack of merit, or with a lack of any kind.

In spite of the small voice that was telling me the work may have been formed incorrectly, I liked the substance of what I had written. A few of my students, like Tisch Jones who directed the play, also liked it; and Bob Hedley, who had hired me for the visiting professorship, told me he especially liked it. Since I'd submitted only one play with my application, I knew it had been on the strength of the writing in *Hot Methuselah* alone that I had been hired for the position. Still, whenever I thought about the play, I would pick it up and reread it, trying to find the flaws; but I could find no skips or jumps. By the fifth line of the play, it was clear what the conflict was. The characters were round and clearly drawn. The storyline was strong. After going over the play with my critical eye, I concluded that nothing was missing, and that much of what had gone wrong with the reading Tisch had put together in the Playwrights Lab had been due to the fact that the work had simply taken the actors by surprise. They'd had no time to *get into* character; they had to *be* in character by the first line of the play. The actors had underestimated the work. I would see this time and again at future productions of the form.

The genre was a challenge...no, a struggle! And I determined to keep wrestling with it until I was certain I had mastered it. To my way of seeing it, I simply had to stay within the boundaries of the ten pages and compress all the elements of the short-short story into the dramatic structure. Furthermore, the work had to draw upon a strong cultural base for its substance and, where possible, move beyond the monologue. I saw how I could draw upon my early relationship with the short story, wed the two genres, and draw upon the voice, rhythm and value system of a rich Black cultural tradition to forge yet another form which I would call *the Ten-Minute folk drama*. Later in the semester, something happened which set me firmly on that course.

The theater department required, as a condition for completion of the MFA program in directing, that its students direct a new work in the Summer Playwrights Festival, and that it be written by someone in the Playwrights Lab. Here Tisch faced a racial barrier. All the playwriting students were White, and none of them wanted to work with a Black director. Tisch went to Bob, who knew what the problem was. And so he stretched the rules by reasoning that, since I was associated with the Playwright's Lab and also with the Iowa Summer Festival as a guest member of the department, a work of mine could be eligible. I knew Tisch was eager to direct in the Ten-Minute genre. The problem was that I had written only one work, and it was not long enough to fill an afternoon or evening slot.

Spring Break was only a few days off. I had to return to New York to see about my daughter, so I told Tisch that during the break I would do my best to work on at least two more pieces I had been mulling over since being in Iowa. When I returned from spring break, I brought with me the first draft of *Two Mens'es Daughter,* the first of my Ten-Minute plays to be published, first by Applause Theater Books, and then by Harcourt Brace in the Seventh Edition of its Perrine's Literature series. A few days after my return to Iowa, I also completed *S'posed-to-Be Daddy.* After meeting with Bob, Tisch told me he had approved the scripts for her project, that he had a lot of questions about *Two Mens'es Daughter*, but that he liked *S'pozed-to-Be Daddy* a lot.

Tisch now had three Ten-Minute plays. The challenge was to stage them in a way which could communicate a unity of theme and purpose. I was not aware that I had written them with any particular unified theme in mind. But one evening, Tisch came to me in a state of excitement. She'd had a revelation: that all three of the plays had a spiritual root, and that she would take them back to the church, where they'd been born. She would link them, she decided, with music. We both began thinking of appropriate music, and almost immediately *Come, Ye Disconsolate* came to mind. There's a line in the song, which goes straight to the heart of the plays: *"Come to the mercy seat."*

I've been asked many times to explain the term. What exactly is *the mercy seat?* I go back in memory to the little Texas community in Houston's Fifth Ward, to the St. Luke's Baptist Church, which I attended in my childhood. There was a bench located up front near the pulpit. Some people called it the *sinner's bench;* some called it *the throne;* still others called it *the mercy seat.* It was all of the above. Over the years, I've come to understand that *the mercy seat* is not only a place in the church, it is a metaphor for a place in the heart. Those who had wronged the community and who sought reconciliation, were invited to *take it to the throne*, approach that bench, confess their trespasses and ask the congregation for forgiveness and mercy. In each play of the decatet, a character is in need of mercy; in each play, the mercy is granted.

I purposely didn't attend any rehearsals of the plays for the Iowa Summer Festival; and on the day the plays were presented, I was stunned by what I saw! And so was everyone else in the audience, including the enemies of the production. Yes, there were enemies of the production.

I hadn't noticed that all of the plays were inter-generational, but Tisch had noticed. She had a difficult task, but she found real elders from the Iowa community to play the elder roles. Another of my students, Leonard Curtis, had designed a minimalist set, which had the feel of a church. The flow of the plays was astonishingly even and seamless from beginning to the very end. Tisch had found the spiritual center of all the plays, and when the performance was over, there was barely a dry eye in the theater.

This was truly a Eureka experience for me. I had not only found my signature work, I had found a director who could conceptualize how to make it work.

I kept on writing in the genre until I had ten plays. I thought this was a good place to round them off as a set, and so I called the set of ten *a decatet*. The following year, I wrote ten more. The second decatet, entitled *Grey Panthers: Precious Memories*, focuses on African-American historical personalities who boldly confronted the political forces of their day and who left us the benefit of their wisdom in overcoming these forces. Both decatets have at their center feisty elders, gray-haired characters asserting their rights—grey panthers—and steering the plays toward their resolution.

The first decatet explores the role of mercy in resolving conflicts between individuals; and so I titled the set *GREY PANTHERS: Coming to the Mercy Seat*. When James Lincoln directed seven plays from the first decatet at Grinnell College in Grinnell, Iowa, he described them as being about "the pain of loving someone." I was very reluctant to go and see the Grinnell production because I didn't believe the casting across ethnic lines, especially with student actors, would work. But I was wrong. James had cast Latino students, Black students, and White students with Appalachian accents and latex makeup to age them; and when I sat in the back of the theater and closed my eyes, I couldn't detect the age of the actor, and barely the ethnicity.

Years later, when Tisch directed some of the works at The Old Creamery in Garrison, Iowa, she noted, "Though the pieces were written in a culture-specific and age-specific framework, the rural settings, the inter-generational relationships, and the themes of joy and sorrow are truly universal. People identify with the situations and emotions beyond race and age."

My third decatet, entitled *Sons...and Fathers of Sons*, is an all-male cast set which deals with father-son relationships; my fourth decatet deals with mother-daughter relationships; my fifth decatet deals with Race and Racism.

I just keep following the spirit!

J. e Franklin, New York City, 2003

A DIRECTOR'S NOTES

BACKGROUND

Grey Panthers: Coming to the Mercy Seat came into my life as a blessing. It was January of 1990, and J. e Franklin had just been hired as a visiting professor in the department of theater arts at the University of Iowa, where I was a student working on my master's degree. We were two black women on a campus where there were very few black students.

My final semester of graduate school was overwhelmingly difficult and challenging, but having J. e Franklin as the teacher of my graduate script analysis course was one of the perks. Getting a glimpse of her theoretical approach to script analysis gave me insight into the grounding of her work. At that time, she was experimenting with the ten-minute play form. When I read her *Hot Methuselah*, I enjoyed it so much, I asked the head of the department to allow me to present a public reading of it at the weekly theatre lab for faculty and students. When the play was presented, students and faculty were quite surprised at how many emotions could be explored in such a short time. Some of the students had an awakening when they realized that someone black had been invited to join Iowa's teaching staff, not to fulfill affirmative action guidelines, but because she was a good artist, and an established one, as well.

At mid-semester, each student in the graduate directing program is required to direct a new work by an Iowa playwriting student whose work would be presented during the spring semester in a much-acclaimed Playwrights Festival, where invited guests in the theatre world are brought in for feedback. The problem was that all of the playwriting students in the program were white, and they had all paired off with white directors. As the outsider, there was no way for me to fulfill the requirements for my degree. I asked my advisors Eric Forsythe and Bob Hedley if I would be penalized for not being able to fulfill the requirements, and they promised to help me find a new work to direct. Knowing how excited I was about *Hot Methuselah* and the ten-minute form, I asked if the new work could be by J. e Franklin. The problem was that J. e had only one ten-minute play, but seeing the predicament I was in, she promised to work on at least two more during the upcoming spring break. True to her word, she returned from the break with *S'pozed-to-Be Daddy,* and *Two Mens'es Daughter*. These three works formed the beginnings of what would eventually become a body of inter-generational, elder-centered Ten-Minute plays---ten in the set--- which J. e would entitle: Grey Panthers, Coming to the Mercy Seat.

PROCESS

In April of 1990, we started rehearsing the three plays: *Hot Methuselah, Two Mens'es Daughter, and S'pozed-to-be Daddy*. Very early in the process, it became obvious that the theme of redemption was at the heart of all three plays. The concern was how to connect all three plays as a complete work instead of as three separate works. The designer, Leonard Curtis, suggested three areas on separate platforms completely furnished as separate units. The performing spaces would be positioned in a semi-circle to provide a sense of unity. In rehearsing the early drafts of the script, the actors and I explored the musicality of the language and the visual life of the characters. The more we worked, the more we realized that music would be the great unifier of this work. I asked J. e what song reflected her sense of the three plays, and she suggested "Come, Ye Disconsolate." Having grown up with that song, I quickly sat at the piano and began playing this old, familiar hymn. We both agreed that we needed a wonderful rendition of the song. I had the Hubert Laws rendition, which was a beautiful and graceful jazz flute instrumental. Though wonderful, it was not correct for our production. Finally, J. e suggested the Roberta Flack-Donny Hathaway rendition. This was the perfect music for our production, but how could we find a copy of it in Iowa? We were not able to secure a copy of the record until the final dress rehearsal, which was held the morning of the opening.

The actors knew their lines and had developed quite wonderful characters, considering their age range. Since this was a university production, finding age-appropriate black actors on this Iowa campus was a challenge. Our search took us outside the university area, and even with this search, the age range of our cast was nineteen to forty. Also, since the role of Aunt Goldie in *Two Mens'es Daughter* required an actor who could pass for white, we were able to use a white faculty member.

From the moment I heard the first chords to the opening lines of the Flack-Hathaway song, I knew I had found the key to the staging. The strong pulse of the instrumental behind the words reminded me of the black choirs I had grown up with. The music finally connected me to J. e's roots and the similarity of our southern backgrounds. The concept of the work had at its heart the need to bring the audience to *the mercy seat*.

In the last moments of rehearsal, I tried to incorporate this late discovery but knew realistically that I would have to wait until future productions to incorporate these new revelations. It was too late to strip the set of all the furniture. All that could be imposed on the process that day was to work on the entrance of all the characters at the top of the play. This was the beginning of a gospel march entrance for all the characters who needed to give witness to their joys and pain.

As the year progressed, J. e continued to write more ten-minute plays. On my 42nd birthday, J. e gave me the first draft of *The Closer The Kin*. When she wrote the tenth play, she named the set The First Decatet. We finally had an opportunity to do a reading of the new plays at the Louis Abrons Arts Center in New York. That was when I found a way to use only one chair for each of the plays. At this point, we had the opportunity to use age-appropriate actors, which brought greater depth to the overall work. At the end of a well-received evening, I realized the power of using one chair. That one chair represented the mercy seat mentioned in the song, "Come, Ye Disconsolate." From that moment on, the central focus of Grey Panthers became "coming to the mercy seat." It was J. e who suggested the chair should be a rocking chair, since the rocker is such a great soother; thus, "the mercy seat."

Some months later, we had an opportunity to stage the work at the Langston Hughes Theater in Harlem's world-famous Schomburg Center for Research in Black Culture. Ruby Dee and Ossie Davis moderated this ground-breaking presentation, which was followed by a community folk-talk.

It was evident that all the production elements had worked well, and that through the characters, the audience had identified with the conditions, issues and pressures in their own lives. The power of the work had turned the evening into a Monday night community church meeting. This was Grey Panthers at its final hour. Not only did the work move the audience to bear witness to their own lives and to the lives of those in their communities, the opportunity to talk back served as a balm. Thus the idea of the Folk-Talk as Second Act was born.

REFLECTIONS

September 18, 2003. I sat in a Chicago airport, amazed at the body of work developed by this playwright, whose initial motive for exploring the form was to help her student fulfill the requirements of a degree. J. e has since written five decatets.

Other directors have directed works from them, and I have directed many productions of them at universities, social clubs, libraries, churches and theaters across the country.

Thirteen years have passed since the first presentation of Grey Panthers in Iowa. What worked then is still in order:

Use only one chair. Think church. Think community outreach. Think of the Second Act as the audience's time to participate. Do no more than five plays. In my experience, more than five is too much pain for the audience.

Though Ruby and Ossie set a precedent as celebrity moderators of the audience feedback, it is best to involve members of the community: ministers, teachers, social workers, etc., as facilitators. It is best not to use the playwright, the actors or any other production staff for the Folk-Talk. The dialogue should focus on the issues raised in the plays, on the lessons the community learned, and on how the community may foster answers and support for such problems.

With the publication of this decatet, there will be more productions of Grey Panthers. Believe me, every community, regardless of ethnicity or gender, will benefit from the experience.

Tisch Jones, Associate Professor
Department of Theatre Arts
The University of Iowa

Professor Tisch Jones is a teacher and director. She has taught at Spelman College and the University of Northern Iowa. She has directed at The Apollo Theater, The New Federal Theater, The Ellen Stewart Theatre, at Lincoln Center Theater in New York City, and at The Kennedy Center in Washington, D. C.

J.e Franklin

Tuckin,' pleatin,' folding's what he did
Pouncing on girls that ain't nothing but kids.

"Mama, let's go!
Let me carry your bags.
You don't need to be with him
Turning into no old hag."

May/December marriage
Grandpa said it wouldn't work
Daddy's cheatin' ways
Got you all embarrassed and hurt

That old fool!
That Hot Methuselah.

N'zinga

Coming To The Mercy Seat

HOT METHUSELAH

J.e Franklin

CHARACTERS IN ORDER OF APPEARANCE

ALICE WILKINS, 65 plus

CHARLES WILKINS, 30

RICHARD WILKINS, Methuselah

Coming To The Mercy Seat

ALICE, angry and determined, is stuffing her suitcase to capacity.

CHARLES enters, treading lightly.

CHARLES
Aw, mama, please don't do this...!

ALICE
You just stay out-a this.

CHARLES
Stay out...? You and Joyce are the ones mixing me up in it...she come calling me on my job telling me to come see 'bout you.

ALICE
I ain't told her to send nobody to see 'bout me.

CHARLES
Well, mama, what did you expect her to do when you called her all upset?

ALICE
I should-a knew better'n to call her!

CHARLES
Daddy in there with his head all hung down...

ALICE
He ought-a hang his head.

CHARLES
Joyce told me what he did, but you don't have to leave like this.

ALICE
I don't need you to tell me what I don't have to do.

CHARLES
Mama, I don't blame you for being mad, but you'll hurt him more by staying here and making him look you in the face every day. You got something to hold over him now. Just throw it up in his face now and then, and make him feel guilty.

ALICE
You just don't know your daddy…he'll go off and get him a cigar and play like he deaf-and-dumb.

CHARLES
What's me and Joyce suppose to tell our friends?

ALICE
Tell 'em the truth.

CHARLES
Tell 'em our daddy was down on Pearl Harbor "slumming," and the bus passed by with our mama on it?

Coming To The Mercy Seat

ALICE
You ain't got to say all that.

CHARLES
Then tell me what we should say so one won't be saying one thing and the other another thing.

ALICE
Can't y'awl use y'awl's heads for more 'n a hat-rack? Just say we're separated.

CHARLES
This don't even make no sense. If this was the first time daddy had did something like this, I could understand you being upset but you knew he was looking at other women.

ALICE
You can call it looking if you want to, but what I seen was more 'n looking. He has that heiffer penned against the side-a that Deluxe Theater like he was fixing to ram her through the wall.

CHARLES
Ram her with what?! What can daddy do with a woman?

ALICE
Plenty, to let him tell it.

CHARLES
Aw, what man don't think he's the cock of the barnyard? I'm surprised daddy could even see the woman.

ALICE
He seen her, all right! Think he gonna bring a outside baby here for me to raise like your Uncle John did your Aunt Ruth but he got another thought coming.

CHARLES
A baby?! Mama, please! Daddy can't give no woman no baby!

ALICE
That's what you think. Wasn't Abraham up in age when he begat Ishmael by Hagar, then took him home for Sarah to raise?

CHARLES
That was back in Bible-days, mama...men ain't up to what they was back then.

ALICE
Yes, they is, too...they up to the same old low-down ways.

CHARLES
I didn't mean it in that sense.

ALICE
That thing don't have to be working a hundred percent for some thing to happen, you know... you made it here.

Coming To The Mercy Seat

CHARLES
Mama, I hate to say this, but by you letting daddy get away with this all these years, you helped bring it to this. If you had-a sic'ed your vengeful hounds on him from the git-go, you could-a nipped it in the bud.

ALICE
How you know what I could-a done? Yeah, I used to give him a quarter or two and let him go buy him some. He wasn't gonna wear me out! But he never did it right under my nose before.

CHARLES
He wasn't trying to do it under your nose, mama. The bus wasn't even supposed to go down Lyons Avenue, but they had that big fire on Market Street.

ALICE
I seen it, just the same, and Sister Gertie was on that bus, and she seen it, too.

CHARLES
Old Gravel Gertie? Oh, Lord! I bet the whole town gonna know 'bout it now!

ALICE
That's what was so killing about it. I believe I could'a lived with it if it'd just been me seen it. But to have my friends and neighbors see it...

CHARLES
Well, you ain't making it no better, walking out the

door with this big-fat suitcase. Every window-raising granny 'round here gonna be peeping from behind their window shades.

ALICE
Let 'em peep...you just come here and help me shut this thing.

CHARLES
You got too much in it. I can see that from 'way over here.

ALICE
It'll shut. I'll sit on it and you lock it.

>   (ALICE sits on the suitcase as her son struggles to lock it.)

CHARLES
Mama, you gotta take something out-a here 'fore you tear this old piecy thing. I can hear it cracking.

ALICE
Oh, all right.

>   (ALICE takes a few things from the suitcase. CHARLES notices a photograph.)

CHARLES
Hey! Who did this! Who cut this picture up like this?

Coming To The Mercy Seat

ALICE
Don't you worry about it.

CHARLES
Mama, you did this? Cut daddy out from next to me at my graduation and got him looking like the headless horseman?

ALICE
He was standing next to me, too, and I'm getting particular 'bout who I take a picture with.

CHARLES
Aww, ain't this something?! You done messed the picture up! It don't even look right now!

ALICE
You ain't gotta look at it ...just put it back where you found it... it wasn't bothering you.

CHARLES
You think you can cut almost forty years of marriage out-a your life with a pair scissors?

ALICE
Boy, don't you come in here questioning me like you Perry Mason or something. What do you know 'bout any years of marriage? You ain't been married barely going on two months.

CHARLES
I guess I don't know nothing.

ALICE
You just make sure you don't get caught down on Pearl Harbor.

CHARLES
I ain't lost nothing down there.

ALICE
...ought-a be thinking 'bout being some kind-a monk or some thing at his age...I didn't even know he still wanted pussy.

CHARLES
Mama! I ain't never heard you talk like that!

ALICE
Well...you grown now...you old enough to know of these things.

CHARLES
I knew of those things before I was grown, but even at that...

ALICE
You wasn't supposed to know of 'em. Smelling your nature 'fore your time, that's what...like father, like son.

CHARLES
If Rev. Hill heard you talking like this...!

Coming To The Mercy Seat

ALICE
Humph! If what Sister Hill told me about him is true...and I don't believe she'd lie on him...he bet ' not come trying to preach no sermon to me. The monkey don't never see his own ass!

CHARLES
This thing shore must be hurting you to your heart, cause I ain't never heard you talk like this.

ALICE
My heart ain't your worry.

CHARLES
Well, daddy shore been worried about your heart, cause he talked to me about it. He said you been round here taking heart medicine and didn't want me and Joyce to know. That could-a been why daddy did what he did, not wanting to give you no heart attack.

ALICE
My heart would-a made it through all that tucking and pleating and folding he do.

CHARLES
Well, see there? The old gray mare ain't what he used to be so what could he-a done with a woman?

ALICE
I'm surprised at you taking up for him. Who could beat you running from him when you was little? Hiding all under the bed when he came in here raising cain?

CHARLES
I forgive him, mama. And you used to say "kill a dog with kindness." Now just look at you.

ALICE
Well..do as I say do..don't do as I do.

CHARLES
It don't work like that cause I didn't wanna tell you but... me and Noreen.

ALICE
What about you and Noreen?

CHARLES
We ain't making it.

ALICE
Don't tell me she caught you down on Pearl Harbor, too.

CHARLES
Now, see there? How come it always gotta be the man that's doing wrong? Can't a woman do wrong, too?

ALICE
She can if she did...did she?

CHARLES
I found a telephone number in her pocketbook.

Coming To The Mercy Seat

ALICE
What was you doing going in her pocketbook?

CHARLES
That ain't the point...

ALICE
It is the point. You and your daddy is always looking for cow-shit where the cow ain't even grazed yet. My Cousin Henry gave me a ring his wife wanted me to have before she died and your daddy come digging all in my pocketbook and running up in my face with it...

CHARLES
I gotta wait till the cow come in my pasture 'fore I see him? And, mama, why you gotta cuss like that?

ALICE
Plug your ears up if you don't wanna hear it. Y'awl ain't running my life no more.

CHARLES
I'm not trying to run your life, mama.

ALICE
I been on my feet all day long, my corns killing me... in and out-a them dev'lish stores trying to find some decent drawers to go on your daddy's raggedy-ass, and he somewhere trying to take the drawers off some chippy! Then tried to plant that Judas-kiss on me when he crept in the door.

CHARLES
As pitiful as he looking in there now, seem like you could just whip his behind and that 'd be the end of it.

ALICE
I'm scared I'd break some-a his old dry bones, then the sheriff'll put me under the jail, 'stead-a in it.

CHARLES
Where you gonna stay? Me and Noreen can get a roll-away bed. You know what grandpa gonna say if you go out there. He didn't want you to marry no man that old, nohow.

ALICE
I don't know what make you think I'm gonna go running to my daddy and to you, neither. I got plenty places to go and I ain't gonna be backed up in some old roach-corner, neither.

CHARLES
All right, mama.

ALICE
Come here and see if it'll shut now.

>(CHARLES takes his time closing the suitcase.
>
>ALICE falls into a mood, her anger spent.)

Coming To The Mercy Seat

CHARLES
I know as soon as we step out that door Old Gravel Gertie n'em's shades gonna fly up. I can just see 'em, their tongues just a-wagging like they ain't got nothing better to do than sit at them windows and wait for something to gossip about. Mama, I was thinking, maybe if I take the suitcase like it's mine and drive off, then come back later for you...

>(ALICE does not answer...just rocks herself.)

ALICE
If it had-a been a woman more my age, it wouldn't-a been so bad, but that girl was young enough to be his great, great grandgirl.

CHARLES
A girl?!

ALICE
Look like that child you brought here one time.

CHARLES
Who? Couldn't-a been nobody I know.

ALICE
That child-who-her-mama-wasn't-right-in-the-head. Yes it was her, too...it's coming back to me!

CHARLES
Phila Mae? You talking about Phila Mae?

ALICE
I knew I seen that child before. Didn't she go to school with you?

CHARLES
She went to school with me but you couldn't-a seen her down on no Pearl Harbor.

ALICE
Don't tell me what I didn't see. I just couldn't feature her at first, but it was her all right.

CHARLES
What was she doing down there?

ALICE
The same thing all the rest'a them hot'tail heiffers was doing and she was doing it with that daddy of yours.

CHARLES
Why, that hoary-headed, horny old Methuselah! My girlfriends used to tell me he'd be winking and going on at them when I'd bring them here and I didn't believe them! I ought-a go in there and give him a piece-a my mind!

ALICE
You ain't gotta tell him nothing. Let him have the pussy I got the money!

CHARLES
And just look at how he got you talking! I'm mad now! Did you give him that underwear? I hope you didn't

Coming To The Mercy Seat

give him nothing.

ALICE
I started to take 'em back and get my money back but I didn't.

CHARLES
Are they Fruit-of-the-Loom? Cause I need some.

ALICE
I reckon they fruit-a something.

CHARLES
Let's go, mama. I got my car...where you wanna go?

ALICE
You just hold your mule. Set my bag back down there. I ain't asked you to car'y me nowhere.

CHARLES
You gonna let him get away with this when he knew better?

ALICE
How you know he knew better? How you know he ain't senile?

CHARLES
If a man still got that on his mind he ain't all that senile.

ALICE
You just skin your cat and let me skin mine.

CHARLES
All right, mama...I was just trying to help.

(RICHARD enters, and when ALICE sees her husband's bent, contrite form, her anger is abated, but CHARLES remains unforgiving.)

RICHARD
Babe...you gonna leave me some money for my cigars 'fore you go?

(ALICE averts her eyes, hesitates, but soon yields.)

ALICE
Hand me my purse over there, boy.

(Her son starts to protest, but a hard look from ALICE changes his mind. She fumbles in her purse, takes out the money for her husband.)

ALICE
You reckon this gonna be enough?

RICHARD
Yeah, that's enough...that's enough. Thank you babe. Thank you.

(He tries to hold onto her hand, but she yanks it away. As RICHARD shuffles out, ALICE weeps softly.)

Coming To The Mercy Seat

                    ALICE
Old fool!

            (CHARLES goes to her side.)

                    CHARLES
Aw, mama, it's gonna be all right. Mama, don't cry.
Please, don't cry.

            (The LIGHTS go out to end the action.)

                    <u>**END**</u>

J.e Franklin

They say the closer the kin,
The deeper in.

This bond, tighter than most sometimes.
He learns from her
How to treat a woman
How a woman feels...

She learns from him
What a man is all about
Maybe helps him get there.

They say, "Tell me your secret
And I'll tell you mine."
His boys holla' at him,
"Man, your sister, she's hot!"

Her girls holla' back,
"Girl, your brother, he's fine!"
They see finally what others see...
But refuse.

How far will it go
This bond, too deep, too strong?
The closer the kin...

N'zinga

Coming To The Mercy Seat

THE CLOSER THE KIN

J.e Franklin

CHARACTERS IN ORDER OF APPEARANCE

Cora Bellins, 65 plus

Preston Bellins, 75 plus

Coming To The Mercy Seat

A bench or a rocking chair is all there is of a set.

CORA is seated, stringing beans.

PRESTON enters, visibly unsettled.

CORA
Hey'dere...thought I heard you come in. How's Lena doing?

PRESTON
Well...she ain't doing too good...and I told her I was gonna try to get her out-a there.

CORA
Preston, why do you tell her things to get her hopes up?

PRESTON
Well, I...I kind-a told her she was coming home.

CORA
Coming to what home? Preston, don't you start this foolishness!

PRESTON
Cora, she was crying her eyes out...

CORA
I knew she was gonna get you out there and pull that crying act!

PRESTON
She wasn't acting no such-a thing. I know when my sister

is hurting...them people is mistreating her.

CORA
Ain't nobody doing nothing to her! That place came highly recommended...

PRESTON
I don't care how high it recommended. I ain't leaving my sister in no old folk's home.

CORA
Preston, you can't bring her here, and that's that!

PRESTON
How come you can bring your people here when they on they ass, but I can't bring mine here?

CORA
What *my* people? If you talking 'bout Dee-Dee...

PRESTON
That's exactly who I'm talking about!

CORA
Dee-Dee got around here and ironed and cooked and cleaned...

PRESTON
She was supposed to do something...'round here eatin' my food! I had to tell her to stop propping her filthy feet up in that ice box...

CORA
What...?

Coming To The Mercy Seat

PRESTON
Don't act like you don't know about it! I told you how she'd come in that kitchen two-three o'clock in the morning, pull up a chair to that ice box and prop her feet up in it, then eat up everything she could get her hands on, beans, greens...everything!

CORA
My sister might-a had her ways...

PRESTON
Ain't no *might-a* to it!

CORA
One thing about it, Dee Dee could wipe her own ass. Lena's so crippled up with that arthur'itis, you know she can't even wipe her ass, Preston!

PRESTON
I ain't asked you to wipe it, did I?

CORA
Then who's gonna do it? 'Cause I'm telling you right now, I ain't wiping nobody's ass but my own!

PRESTON
I can hire a woman to help her.

CORA
Preston, Lena need twenty-four hour care!

PRESTON
Her social security check'll cover everything, and we can find somebody to live in...

CORA
Preston, for God's sake, where we gonna put two grown people?!

PRESTON
Well, if all that furniture and stuff you keep holding onto wasn't in here...

CORA
Now, I know you done lost your mind, talking 'bout touching my furniture!

PRESTON
You don't even use half-a that junk!

CORA
My furniture ain't going nowhere!

PRESTON
I ain't leaving my sister in no institution!

CORA
That's your privilege, Preston. But this house ain't big enough for me and Lena, and if you bring her here, one of us is gonna have to go, and it ain't gonna be me.

PRESTON
This is my house, too. I worked just as hard as you did to pay for it.

CORA
That don't give you the right to bring people in here to run over me.

Coming To The Mercy Seat

PRESTON
How is my sister gonna run over you, when she can't even walk?

CORA
You know what I mean, Preston. It ain't gonna be nothing but a whole lot-a mess, just like it was when she moved in with us before….and whose side did you always take?

PRESTON
You provoked her as much as she provoked you.

CORA
Preston…I thought after the children got up some size, we could have these few years we got left all to ourselves.

PRESTON
What kind-a years would they be for me when all my boyhood friends is dead and gone? Lena's the only family I got left from my youth, Cora…

CORA
But why me? Why ask me to carry her cross when she didn't even want me to marry you?

PRESTON
I know y'awl never got along…but what can she do to you now that she's flat on her back?

CORA
The same thing she did to your cousin Patty and to your mother—two good women put in the ground before their time for waiting on her hand and feet.

J.e Franklin

PRESTON
My mama owed Lena plenty for dumping us on our auntie when we was kids. Hadn't been for Lena scrubbing floors and toilets and eating left'overs off the white folk's tables, we wouldn't-a even ate. Lena would drink bacon grease and give me the food. That's why she's in that chair right today. And as for Patty Lee, Jack Daniel put her in the ground. She's the one tricked Lena into that damn place.

CORA
She pretend to have so much sense, so how did that happen? You can't smell her shit, but I heard the way she used to talk to y'awl's mama, and I knew God wasn't gonna let her walk again. Naw, it wasn't right for your mama to go off and leave y'awl like that, but she was still y'awl's mother.

PRESTON
I don't care what nobody say. I seen all kind-a low stuff in this world and my sister ain't no worse than nobody else. If God *is* punishing her, then He ain't all He's trumped up to be. Foxes got dens...the buzzard got a nest... yet my sister can't have no home to lay her head?

CORA
She got a right to the tree-a life, but I don't owe her nothing! And I'm tired, Preston! What about Essie Mae? Wasn't she looking for a boarder?

PRESTON
I asked her...she say she want a settle'man.

CORA
Too bad Lena never had children.

Coming To The Mercy Seat

PRESTON
If they'd turned out like ours did, they wouldn't be worth a damn. Look at how much they auntie did for them boys. You'd think one of 'em would let they auntie come there.

CORA
The boys got families of their own to look after.

PRESTON
Everybody just done turn't they back on my sister. Ain't nothing for me to do but go'on back out to the farm and take her with me.

CORA
Fool, have you completely lost your mind? What you gonna do when it get cold, with that piecy roof and the whole place leaning like it's ready to fall?

PRESTON
Somebody'll help me fix it.

CORA
Who, Preston? Everybody out there is as old as you!

PRESTON
I'll find somebody.

CORA
You couldn't even get nobody to help you put up a picket fence!

PRESTON
Then I'll do it myself, woman!

CORA
You'll go up on that rotten roof by yourself!
Preston, please hush this foolishness!

PRESTON
I promised God that if He let me live to be a man, I was gonna look after my sister as long as I had two good hands and two good feet.

CORA
You ain't but two good feet from death's door! And what about the promise you made to me? You told that preacher you would forsake all others and cling to me.

PRESTON
And you promised to be my helpmeat!

CORA
Are you saying I ain't been a good wife to ya?

PRESTON
Up to now you been a good one, and I'm asking you to go all the way with me, Cora.

CORA
I stuck by you through all your foolish schemes that never went nowhere...I washed the shit off the walls when you came in drunk and missed the toilet...

PRESTON
I said you been a good wife to me, but blood is thicker than water, Cora!

CORA
Am I the water, Preston?

Coming To The Mercy Seat

PRESTON
You asking me to turn my back on somebody I sopped from the same dish with.

CORA
You sopped from my dish. I gave you five sons! But I guess what you got from me wasn't good enough to you.

PRESTON
Cora, I'm just going to look after my sister, and you trying to find something wrong in it.

CORA
I'm not trying to find wrong, I'm reminding you that I'm your wife. But this is your choice, so you do the choosing.

PRESTON
I'm not choosing.

CORA
Yes, you are, Preston. You married *me*, but like they always say, "The closer the kin, the deeper in."

PRESTON
Aw, git your mind out the gutter!

CORA
I'm your second wife...Lena's your first wife.

PRESTON
Cut it out, Cora!

CORA
People shore used to whisper about it. Your own cousin Patty used to say you'd eat ten yards-a Lena's shit...

    (PRESTON, shaking with rage, raises his hand to strike.)

PRESTON
Dog'gone you! I'll slap you into hell!

CORA
That's right! Bring down that hand and draw back a nub! I ain't never seen you raise your hand to Lena!

PRESTON
I don't wanna hurt you, Cora, but I swear to God, if you keep this up...!

CORA
You and Lena think everything is about y'awl. Well, I got needs, too. I'm hurting, too, Preston!

PRESTON
You ain't hurting like Lena is hurting. You can walk! How you think my sister feel all these years, watching people walking and running and she gotta wait for somebody to come be her feet?

CORA
Is that my fault, Preston? Am I my brother's keeper?

PRESTON
You shore got people at that church *thinking* you some kind-a saint. Just let a stranger stump his toe and off you go running to see about him! All I asked you to do was just

Coming To The Mercy Seat

do for my sister what you would want done for you, and you won't even slack the rope around her neck! Well, I don't care if it rain inside and leak outdoors, I rather eat dry bread in a shack than be here with you. Who know if you won't have me put away if I get so I can't do for myself.

      (PRESTON heads out, but
      CORA stops him.)

        CORA
Preston, wait! Don't do this. Don't leave without helping me work this out. I never left you...and I got my pride, too!

        PRESTON
I just can't find it in my heart to leave her like this, Cora, 'cause I know she wouldn't'a left me in no place like that.

        CORA
Then let me go out to the farm and you stay here with Lena.

        PRESTON
Let *you* go? Now who's sounding like a fool?!

        CORA
If Lena come here, I'm gonna leave anyhow, so just let me go now.

        PRESTON
You know you can't make it out there by yourself.

        CORA
People will help a woman quicker than they'll help a man.

PRESTON
How's that gonna look? Me sitting in a warm house, and you in a cold shack?

CORA
Don't worry about me...I'll be all right.

PRESTON
How'm I gonna keep from worrying about ya?

CORA
'Cause I said don't worry.

PRESTON
Babe...you ain't even gotta do this...them boys got room.

CORA
I don't wanna bother the boys. Hush, now!

PRESTON
It just seem like three grown people ought'a be able to work things out. If something was to happen to Dee Dee, I would open my arms to her...

CORA
I know you would....just gimme a little more time to wrestle with this.

PRESTON
Babe...you a good woman. I always tell folks I got a good woman.

CORA
I know you do.

Coming To The Mercy Seat

PRESTON
It just ain't in me to do this no other way.

(PRESTON breaks down in tears, and CORA comforts him.)

CORA
Hush, now...hush now...

<u>END</u>

J.e Franklin

He's still "big pimping"
With that young thang on his arm
Well, his young thang done left
With his young son.

Now his buddy Left Shoe is
Wrestling to get his gun.
Don't want no trouble.
Just get the gun...

N'zinga

Coming To The Mercy Seat

LEFT SHOE'S BUDDY

J.e Franklin

CHARACTERS IN ORDER OF APPEARANCE

WOLFIE, 65 plus

LEFT SHOE, 65 plus

Coming To The Mercy Seat

> The action begins with
> WOLFIE loading his gun.
> He is consumed with hate.
>
> LEFT SHOE enters in time
> to see WOLFIE slip the gun
> into his pocket.

LEFT SHOE
Oh, so you packing a pistol now, huh, Wolfie? And you a deacon in the church! You supposed to set a example...

WOLFIE
I don't need you to come over here preaching to me, Left Shoe. I called you to ask if you would drive me somewhere.

LEFT SHOE
I'm not taking you nowhere with no pistol!

WOLFIE
Then lend me the car, and I'll drive myself.

LEFT SHOE
Not in my car, you ain't! I told you over the phone to let them kids go. What kind-a friend would I be to help you in this? If I drive you down there to kill them kids, that's the same as me killing 'em, and that'd be wrong, Wolfie! It'd be wrong in the eyes of God and wrong in the eyes of man! Let 'em go. This world is full'a women! You can get you another one.

WOLFIE
I don't want n'ary n'other'n! I don't even wanna see no more'a them waenches! After I kill this one, all of 'em can go

to hell!

LEFT SHOE
Kneel with me, Wolfie...let's you and me kneel and pray on this.

WOLFIE
Kneel, nothing! Pray for that waench...she the one need it. I done told you what I need from you. Either you gonna do it or you ain't.

LEFT SHOE
I'll make a deal with you...let me have your pistol, and I'll take you where you wanna go.

WOLFIE
Naw, I ain't giving you my gun.

LEFT SHOE
Then that's it!

WOLFIE
I would do this for you.

LEFT SHOE
Naw, you wouldn't. How many times have you stopped me from doing something I'd be sorry about for the rest-a my life? I let you stop me.

WOLFIE
You don't know what all that waench done did to me!

LEFT SHOE
I heard some-a what's being said on the streets.

Coming To The Mercy Seat

WOLFIE
You knew what had been going on behind my back and you wouldn't come tell me about it.

LEFT SHOE
Wolfie, I told you to keep your eyes open!

WOLFIE
Well, that wasn't telling me nothing. You should'a just came on out and told me who she was fooling with.

LEFT SHOE
How could I tell you to watch your own son!?

WOLFIE
I would-a told you.

LEFT SHOE
Maybe you would'a and maybe you wouldn't'a. Put yourself in my shoes, 'cause don't nobody wanna be the cause of breaking up no family.

WOLFIE
I knew I couldn't satisfy her the way she needed it, but I told her if she was gonna do something, just don't bring it up in my face...respect me with it. You hear what I'm saying, Left Shoe?

LEFT SHOE
Yeah, Wolfie, I hear you...but you keep saying *she-she* and *her-her*. What about Stump? You think he didn't know what he was doing?

J.e Franklin

WOLFIE
Aw, anybody can make a fool out-a Stump. Even when he was a kid, he ain't never had good sense...he just weak to that, 'cause his mama raised him!

LEFT SHOE
Now, you see there, Wolfie? There you go again...always making excuses for Stump.

WOLFIE
You know your horse, I know my mule!

LEFT SHOE
That's why I didn't wanna say nothing. 'Cause to you, the sun rise and set on that boy's head. But mighty funny he gamble, and he shore know how to count his money good!

WOLFIE
I ain't killing my son over no waench! I said if a woman did me wrong again, I wasn't gonna kill the man this time...I said next time, I was gonna kill the woman.

(A beat. LLEFT SHOE is stunned.)

LEFT SHOE
You killed a man, Wolfie? You never told me that before.

(WOLFIE realizes his slip of the lip too late. This has an unsettling affect on LEFT SHOE.)

WOLFIE
Nevermind 'bout that. I know who the devil is. A man just can't win when it come to a woman. Things can be going along just fine, and here she come! Just like back in Bible

Coming To The Mercy Seat

days! Hadn't been for that waench mucking 'round with that snake, we could-a lived forever!

LEFT SHOE
I didn't know you had killed a man, Wolfie.

WOLFIE
Over some waench just like this one. I ain't never had no good luck with womens.

LEFT SHOE
You had a good woman, and you left her, Wolfie. You never heard one ugly word uttered against Lillie Mae when you was with her, but I understand...you wanted some-a that *legal tender, and* because I told you to leave that gal alone, you thought *I* wanted her.

WOLFIE
Naw, I didn't think that...

LEFT SHOE
Yes you did, Wolfie, 'cause we almost fell out about it. All I was saying was if a man gonna fool around with a young gal, he gotta take her somewhere off in the country. You can't be waving her in front-a these young bulls!

WOLFIE
What made me think she felt something for me, she told me she rather be a old man's sweet-heart than a young man's fool.

LEFT SHOE
That ain't what she was saying in the street. She just wanted somebody to pay her rent and help take care-a her kid.

J.e Franklin

WOLFIE
I was doing that! I loved that little kid. That's what's hurting me the most...she took Little Peanut, too. That kid was hugging my neck and calling me daddy. I was the one bathing and feeding her. That waench wasn't looking after her...had her all out in the cold, half n'eked.

LEFT SHOE
You divorced a good woman for a dime-a-dance filly you found on the street. Now you want me to drive you down south so you can kill her!

WOLFIE
The only way I won't kill her, she'll have to hide in a sewer!

LEFT SHOE
And spend the rest-a your life behind bars. 'Cause if you cross state lines with that pistol, Wolfie, you know they gonna lock you up!

WOLFIE
I don't care what they do to me. I ain't got nobody, nohow.

LEFT SHOE
You got me. How you think I'm gonna feel knowing you locked up for life, and I can't do nothing to get you out?

WOLFIE
How much more time do I have left, anyway?

LEFT SHOE
God is the time-keeper *and* the avenger. You might not can read that Bible, but you know it. *Vengence is mine!* Sayeth the Lord.

Coming To The Mercy Seat

WOLFIE
We made in His image. Why He put vengeance in our heart if we can't feel it and use it?

LEFT SHOE
Wolfie, I don't know, but who can beat you running round here talking 'bout how good God is!.

WOLFIE
Yeah, I said He's good, but He ain't *all* good! He built a hell just like He built a heaven, and who did He build it for? For them who won't act right, that's who!

LEFT SHOE
You profess to be a Christian who believe Christ came and did away with all that eye for eye business. We old men now, Wolfie. All we got is our grey hairs. These young lions out here done took over from us, just like we took over from the old mens when we was young. Think back on how we used to call the old men *pops* and they would cuss us out. We didn't see the harm in it. Now *we* old and when these boys call me pops, it go all through me! 'Cause that's the turning of the wheel. No one can live on this earth without wounding *somebody*. You have wronged people, and they didn't kill *you* for it. You say you've killed, Wolfie. Don't you wanna take something *clean* back to God now?

(WOLFIE gives up the pistol.)

WOLFIE
I didn't wanna kill that fellow. I was young then, just barely twenty. Me and this gal was shacking up common-law. Peoples had been telling me this man would come to the house when I went to work, but I never could catch 'em at it. One time, he gived her some money to keep for him, and she

spent it. He come to the house to get it one day, and she didn't have it, so he jumped on her, beat her all in the face, stomped on her and broke her ribs, had her bottom lip hanging all down on her chin! She was supposed to been carrying my kid, or so she said it was mines, but when he got through with her...well, I went down to the Do-Drop-Inn, where I knew he hung out, and told him I wanted to speak with him. I wasn't known to carry no pistol or knife or nothing, so he walked out-a the place with me and went into this alley'way. He say, "I know what you wanna talk about."

He ain't acted like he was sorry for what he did or nothing, and that made me madder! I was walking a little piece in front of him. All of a sudden, I swung around and hit him so hard, his eyeball came out the socket. He went down like he was dead, but he wasn't. I grabbed both-a his legs and spread 'em open. Then I stomped all up in him...tore him up! Tears was running down my face 'til the front'a my shirt was soaking wet. I was trembling and crying and kicking 'til I was wore out. He didn't die til about two days later. Then the sheriff come for me. I was working in this blacksmith shop, making horseshoes. I seen the sheriff when he come in...I just kept right on working. He say, "I come to take you in, Julius." I say, "I know...but I ain't going." He say, "Come on, now, Julius. The peoples done sent me to get you, and I gotta take you." I say just like I said the first time, "I ain't going." He pull his pistol out. "Don't make me have'ta shoot ya', Julius," he say. "That's just what you gonna have'ta do, 'cause I ain't going nowhere with you. Go'on shoot me," I say. His hand commenced to trembling. In a little while, he put his pistol back in his holster and says, "All right, Julius...I'm going back and tell the peoples what happened, and if they tell me I have to come back here and take you, it's gonna be woe'be'unto'you!" And he left. He never did come back. It was told to me that the higher up

Coming To The Mercy Seat

peoples told 'em to let me alone, 'cause they found out why I had did what I did. I stayed there in that place about three more months, but nobody wouldn't have nothing to do with me. They would point at me and call me Cain. "Yonder go Cain...yonder go a murderer! How do it feel to be a murderer?" and all such as that. I would ask 'em, "How you think it feel if I muck you up?!" I stayed there a little bit longer...then I left.

(A beat)

LEFT SHOE
I never killed nobody...not even when I was in the army.

WOLFIE
I don't wanna kill nobody else...but this waench...it wasn't enough she took every stick-a furniture, and got the place so empty, I can hear my echo, but I found out them papers she had me sign wasn't no adoption papers on Little Peanut...they was to get a damn credit card! Now her and that boy going all 'cross the country charging gas and motel rooms, got them peoples calling me for the money...

LEFT SHOE
I told you to come go to that program with me and take up reading. But I understand...you didn't want nobody to know you couldn't read. Now, look, Wolfie...I'll help you call the credit card company and tell 'em you ain't paying no charges on that card.

WOLFIE
I did that, but they keep calling.

LEFT SHOE
I know this lawyer...he helped me one time.

WOLFIE
She done *dreaned* me dry!

LEFT SHOE
But now you rid of her, Wolfie! Be thankful for that!

WOLFIE
How'm I gonna hold my head up in the street? They out there taking bets on what I'm gonna do.

LEFT SHOE
I bet they saying it's a honor for a man to clean his house of dirt!

WOLFIE
I'm so mad I can't even cry!

LEFT SHOE
Hey, Wolfie... you remember that time you and me set down in a gully on that big rock and we cried like babies. You remember that?

WOLFIE
Yeah...I 'member that.

LEFT SHOE
Remember what you said then?

WOLFIE
I don't 'member what I said, but I 'member that gulley.

LEFT SHOE
I'll never forget what you said. You said, "A man gotta cry *sometime*, and if we cry it's because men do."

Coming To The Mercy Seat

WOLFIE
I said that?

LEFT SHOE
You said it, all right! And when I went to work the next day, people was asking me what was I so happy about? I told 'em, "A wise man took me to the rock and helped me clean my heart."

WOLFIE
If she just hadn't-a took little Peanut!

LEFT SHOE
It was her kid, Wolfie. Maybe one day the child will come looking for you...things like that happen.

WOLFIE
She might forget me. And now that you know I kilt a man, you might turn your back on me, too.

LEFT SHOE
What I wanna do that for when it could-a been me? Where would I be at now if you hadn't stopped me when I went at that man with that jackknife? I ran after him so hard, my shoe came off! That's when you gave me my nickname...*Left Shoe*. Shoot, I had paid five dollars for them shoes, and you know that was big money back then. You had picked it up and wouldn't give it back to me, and I couldn't run after the guy over all them sharp rocks and that glass barefeeted. I'll love you for that 'til my dying days. You can always come to me and lay your troubles down in my heart. If I got four-bits, you got two. My people will be your people...

(WOLFIE is overcome by tears.

LEFT SHOE embraces him.)

LEFT SHOE
Aw, Wolfie...I ain't never gonna forsake you! We been through muddy water together! You my main buddy...my ace!

<u>END</u>

Coming To The Mercy Seat

I honored her like the Bible says
Honored her to her death
Loved her so much
And waited for her to return it.

Hoping my child-like love
Was enough for both of us.
She loved him more, loved him period!
While I took care of her...

I loved my mother.

                              N'zinga

J.e Franklin

PUTTIN' MAMA IN THE GROUND

Coming To The Mercy Seat

CHARACTERS IN ORDER OF APPEARANCE

Christine, 65 plus

Elwood, 65 plus

(CHRISTINE is dressed in mourning clothes when the action opens, but she is not in a mourning attitude.

ELWOOD enters, mindful of her mood.)

ELWOOD
Christine...

CHRISTINE
Now, here you come in here...!

ELWOOD
Christine, this is the last chance you'll get to view the body...!

CHRISTINE
Elwood, I'm not going! And that's that!

ELWOOD
Do you know what people are out there saying?

CHRISTINE
What do I care what these old dic'ty cut-throats 'round here say? They should hear what I got to say about them!

ELWOOD
If your brother hadn't set this up, wasn't you gonna have some kind-a service, anyway?

CHRISTINE
I was gonna have the kind-a service decent people have, not some funeral-parlor service to put my mama in the fire!

Coming To The Mercy Seat

ELWOOD
The fire thing is afterwards. The service aint gonna be no different from the ones we have in church. Now, I saw the body...your mama's laid out nice.

CHRISTINE
Don't you talk to me about how nice my mama's laid out, when that two-face'ted Judas-coat is fixin' to have her cremated! I told him if he burn my mama up, I wasn't gonna have nothing to do with it!

ELWOOD
You don't have to be involved with the cremation...!

CHRISTINE
I don't never wanna lay eyes on him again in this life or the next!

ELWOOD
All right, Christine! Ha'mercy!

(A beat.)

CHRISTINE
I didn't ask you to come in here, you know.

ELWOOD
Y'awl got me right smack'dab in the middle of this mess!

CHRISTINE
What you doing in the middle when you supposed to be on *my* side?

ELWOOD
I *am* on your side...

CHRISTINE
You ain't acting like it.

ELWOOD
What you want me to do? He's your people!

CHRISTINE
One thing you can do is stop driving him all over town making arrangements to burn my mama up.

ELWOOD
I didn't know what he intended to do 'til he had it all set up...I wouldn't-a took him nowhere if I'd known what he was up to. I would-a told him to get somebody else.

CHRISTINE
What somebody need to do is get me a gun or something to kill him with so I can throw *his* ass in a fiery furnace and send *his* soul to hell!

ELWOOD
What is this you saying, Christine?! You're letting this thing turn you into a opposum...!

CHRISTINE
Don't you understand what a awful disgrace this is!? How can somebody put fire to the flesh that brought 'em into this world?!

ELWOOD
I told you when your mama was in the hospital, you should-a got her to put her final arrangements in writing.

Coming To The Mercy Seat

CHRISTINE
Mama was too sick... her mind had gone by then. She knew years ago I had started paying on a family plot. She was to be laid next to papa.

ELWOOD
That ain't what your brother said she wrote and told him.

CHRISTINE
I ain't never gonna believe my mama told him to throw her in no fire. It's mighty funny he can't find that letter.

ELWOOD
I can tell you one thing for a fact, your brother don't believe in ground-burial. He believe it's a sin to put that much money in the ground.

CHRISTINE
Yeah, he just wanna fill his pockets with the money...I know that snake!

ELWOOD
Your mama left him the money...left him the house, too.

CHRISTINE
I don't care 'bout the house...I got my own house. But I can still put the law on him. I got rights...she was my mama, too.

ELWOOD
Where's the law that says he gotta put your mama in the ground?

(A beat.)

CHRISTINE
I been asking around. They got a law for which, when you wanna stop a devil from doing dirt you can *'junction* him.

ELWOOD
You gonna let your mama's body lay up somewhere 'til you and your brother stop squabbling? You don't know how long the law gonna take, and when all's said and done, you don't know what the law gonna say.

CHRISTINE
I know the law what say, when you walk in the path of righteousness on this earth, you got a right to spend eternity in that Four-gated City, and not be cast in a lake-a fire like some heathen that never knew Jesus.

ELWOOD
I don't think your brother believe there's a heaven or a hell.

CHRISTINE
When he wake up and find his ass in hell, he'll believe then!

ELWOOD
He say everybody go to the same place when they die: right back to the dirt.

CHRISTINE
Now, you see that! What kind'a preacher is it that say there ain't no hell? I'll tell you what kind! The kind that's done divorced a good woman who gave him eight children and raised 'em all up good! The kind that's done married another woman in that little raggedy hole he call a church, and got both women settin' up in there watching him strutt

Coming To The Mercy Seat

the peacock! Got my sister-in-law calling me on the phone, crying her eyes out! I told her if it was me, I'd get up every time he preach and testify to where that devil keep his tail!

ELWOOD
When I was driving him around in the car, he said he was tired of counseling people who done lost their homes and things, from borrowing money for these big funerals. The graveyard used to be the cheapest boardinghouse, but not no more. He said he seen people take their children's money for college and bury the dead with it. "Let the living take care-a the living and the dead take care-a the dead," he said.

CHRISTINE
Now, if that don't sound like a fool talking! How can the dead take care-a the dead?! Whoever heard-a such a thing!?

ELWOOD
I don't like getting mixed up in y'awl's family mess...I'm just telling you what he said...he's your brother.

CHRISTINE
Brother! What kind-a brother he been to me?! You read them letter he wrote to my mama, low'rating me. You call that a brother?

ELWOOD
I told you what I thought about that. I told you he was just answering something your mama had wrote to him about you.

CHRISTINE
My mama was the only one that had a right to say anything about me...she's the one birthed me into this world.

J.e Franklin

ELWOOD
You know what your mama told me one time? That I was too good for you, and you didn't deserve no good husband.

CHRISTINE
When did she tell you that?

ELWOOD
I didn't wanna tell you before we got married.

(A beat.)

CHRISTINE
I know my mama ain't never loved me. Me and Rachel both knew Chuckie was her heart.

ELWOOD
You thought I had something against your mama 'cause I didn't wanna go around her, but Rachel tried to tell you something before she died.

CHRISTINE
Aw...there was always some fool story a'cusing me-a my daddy. Yes, I loved my daddy and took up for him...none-a the rest of 'em would. But I don't believe my mama really thought such low-down dirt!

ELWOOD
Then why didn't she love you, Christine?

CHRISTINE
I don't know. I'm hoping I'll see her again over yonder and she'll tell me. All my life I felt like a motherless child. When she was sick, who stayed with her and looked after her...washed and bathed her...emptied slop jars and bed

Coming To The Mercy Seat

pans, and changed her drawers? Me, that's who!

ELWOOD
I know....I know...

CHRISTINE
I was the one running back and forth out to that hospital...

ELWOOD
I know, I know...

CHRISTINE
They wasn't even half feeding her! They give her some kinda old peas one time, was so hard they was rolling 'round on the plate like peanuts. I'm the one had to go find her some decent food! And she calling for him! He was half way 'cross the country, and didn't even come to see her but once, and took off as soon as he got here.

ELWOOD
I 'member...

CHRISTINE
Then soon as she die, here he come talking 'bout, "What happened to mama's good watch?!" Questioning me like he the sheriff or something!

ELWOOD
Your mama knew you were the one that really loved her.

(A beat.)

CHRISTINE
That's what's so killing about it! I'm the one that loved and stood by her, but she left him everything...even her body!

ELWOOD
Then let him have it, Christine!

(A beat.)

CHRISTINE
If I could just be sure she made it over!

ELWOOD
Her soul's gone home. She's there now. You did right by your mama when she was alive. Say "well done," dear servant, and let her go.

(A beat.)

CHRISTINE
Did he tell you what he was gonna do with the ashes?

ELWOOD
He said you could have them if you wanted them.

CHRISTINE
Old rotten dog! I don't want no jug-a ashes!

ELWOOD
Christine...your mama's gone! You can't bring her back. No matter how you look at it, it's ashes to ashes, dust to dust.

CHRISTINE
She can come back, you know? She can come back to haunt him. You just ask Mother Sampson!

ELWOOD
Let her haunt him. They made the pact with each other...

Coming To The Mercy Seat

CHRISTINE
All my life she treated me like a red-head step-child. I would-a rather been cut with a dagger than to get the tongue-lashing with the mean and vicious things she used to say to me! But Master Chuckie couldn't do no wrong!

ELWOOD
Christine, she can't hurt you no more.

CHRISTINE
She still doing it through him!

ELWOOD
'Cause you letting him hurt you! I had a mule once that kicked me in the behind when my back was turned...

CHRISTINE
A mule?! I bet your behind shore was sore!

ELWOOD
My behind was sore, but my feelings wasn't. After all, he was just a ass!

(A beat.)

CHRISTINE
Mother Sampson told me if I bring her a pair of his drawers, she'd fix him good!

ELWOOD
Now, just listen at yourself! You don't sound no different from your brother!

CHRISTINE
Oh, so you puttin me in the same category with *him*!

ELWOOD
I don't want to. I'm asking you to come go with me so I can pay my last respects to your mother...

CHRISTINE
Just go'on leave me here!

ELWOOD
You know I won't go without you...she ain't none-a my mother!

CHRISTINE
Sometime I wonder if I ever had a mother.

ELWOOD
Come, darling. They're down there taking pictures.

CHRISTINE
I had a nice dress all picked out for mama that I paid $1,100 dollars for at Lord and Taylor's.

ELWOOD
'Leben hundred dollars! That's more than your wedding gown cost!

CHRISTINE
I'm shore taking it to get my money back!

ELWOOD
Damn! She would-a been the best-dressed corpse in that graveyard...!

CHRISTINE
Ain't no telling what kind-a old rag he done put on mama.

Coming To The Mercy Seat

ELWOOD
The outfit look just fine on her. Now, this is the last time you'll see your mother in this world. After the service, the casket will be sealed and the body will be whisked away. You don't have to say nothing to your brother. I'll keep him away from you. You got my word on it. Do this for me, darling.
        (A beat.)

CHRISTINE
How come my heart always gotta be the blanket to cover everybody?

ELWOOD
'Cause you got the warmest blanket. If your mama never knew that, it was her loss, and I'll tell that to The Great Judge at The Judgement Day.

        (ELWOOD comforts CHRISTINE as she weeps.)

CHRISTINE
My po' mama is gone! Even though she didn't love me, I miss her, Elwood.

ELWOOD
Shore, you miss her, but you still got me. I don't care what your mother said, you *do* deserve me. You deserve the best of everything! Now, come on, darling. Let's go say goodbye to your mama.

        (CHRISTINE allows herself to be led out.)

END

J.e Franklin

No job
No house
Don't wanna work
Ain't gonna look

That's my son...
Damn lazy bum!
Two grown men live in dis here house
Ain't no babies here.

Something's gotta give!

N'zinga

Coming To The Mercy Seat

SPANKY'S POP

J.e Franklin

CHARACTERS IN ORDER OF APPEARANCE

Spanky, 30 plus

Cat,   65 plus

Coming To The Mercy Seat

> We see SPANKY slumped in a chair before a TV which he is not really seeing.
>
> CAT enters and goes to the refrigerator. He finds a food container empty and slams the door in anger.

CAT

I buy the food... you eat it. That's pretty good, ain't it? No wonder you don't wanna go nowhere.

> (SPANKY remains zombie-like, as if he hears and sees nothing.)

CAT

Oh, so you just gonna sit there and ain't gonna say nothing, huh?

SPANKY

Sir?

CAT

Why the hell don't you git up off your ass and git you a job or something? Laying up in here all day long, eating up everything you can git your hands on!

(SPANKY does not respond,
and this angers CAT more.)

CAT

Wasn't you supposed to go by that employment office this morning?

SPANKY

I went by there.

CAT

Went by there when?

SPANKY

Went by there this morning...

CAT

You ain't went-by no such-a-thing! Why you lie like that? People done seen you 'way on the other side-a that track with some-a that trash that come here looking for you everyday. How the hell you get money to buy whiskey and you can't buy no food 'round here?

SPANKY

Who say I bought whiskey? They ain't seen me buy nothing.

CAT

Peoples see you out different places drinking all the time. I know ain't nobody keeping you in that shit just out-a the goodness-a their heart.

Coming To The Mercy Seat

(SPANKY's non-responsiveness increases CAT's exasperation.)

CAT
Boy...I'm telling you the truth...this is a damn shame! I ain't never seen nothing like this in my life! You ain't got no job, no wife, no nothing! You probably ain't never even gave no woman no kid. And if that's what's wrong with ya,' you shore didn't git it from *my* side-a the family!

SPANKY
This woman say I got a kid.

CAT
What woman?

SPANKY
Woman I used to fool-with.

CAT
Oh, *she* say you got a kid. What do *you* say?

(Silence from SPANKY.)

CAT
Why'n't you go stay with *her*?

(SPANKY has tuned-out.)

CAT
If you think you gonna lay up here on me and I take

care-a ya,' you got another thought coming, 'cause I don't have it to do. When you first came here, you said you just wanted to stay the weekend...now it's going on three months! If you ain't out-a here by this Monday'coming, I'm setting your shit out in that hallway...and I mean what I say!

    (SPANKY shifts uncomfortably,
    the first pricking.)

        CAT
Did you hear what I say, Spanky?

        SPANKY
I heard you.

        CAT
Why'n the hell don't you say something, then? And turn that damn box off...running up this light bill...you ain't paying nothing on it!

    (SPANKY clicks the remote.)

        CAT
Can't even bring my women here no mo,' you laying up in here! Got that kitchen all mucked up! And you left that black ring in that bathtub this morning when you got through taking a bath, and I had to clean it out 'fore I could take mine. I'm tired-a this shit! I done told you to clean that shit out-a that tub when you get through. That's another reason I want you out-a here...I don't like filth! And gimme my key to that front door!

Coming To The Mercy Seat

SPANKY
Aw, pop...

CAT
Give it here, I say!

SPANKY
I don't have it no more.

CAT
Don't have it no mo'!? What?!

SPANKY
It's around here somewhere...I just misplaced it...it was in my pocket...

CAT
So how the hell did you git back in here this morning when you went out?

SPANKY
The door was...just open.

CAT
It wasn't no *just open* no such-a-thing! You been picking that lock! I knew somebody been fooling with that lock! I got a good mind to go up'side yout head, 'big as you is! You think I won't do it? You don't never git too big for me to whip! Git in there and clean that kitchen up! You left it for me to clean up, but I got news for ya...'

(SPANKY does not stir.)

CAT

Git on up, I say.

SPANKY

I'm gonna clean it up.

(CAT gives SPANKY an open-hand blow to the head, and SPANKY leaps up in surprise.)

CAT

Git up off your trifling ass and git in that kitchen...!

SPANKY

Hey...! Say, pop, what's wrong with you, man! You ain't gotta disrespect me like that! I'm a man just like you...!

CAT

A what?! A *man*?! Don't no *man* still live in his father's house! Don't no *man* suck on no whiskey bottle 'til he lose a good job! I told ya' you was gonna lose that job, didn't I?

(SPANKY turns aside, trapped.)

CAT

Them people gave you all kind-a chances...sent you to that place to dry out...even paid for it...

then took you back on...three times! A *man*! I 'magine if your mama was where you could get to her, you'd be all under *her*! Why'n't you go live with her?

                SPANKY
You didn't wanna live with her...why should I?

                CAT
What? Now, what is this you saying? You saying *I* didn't wanna live with her?

                SPANKY
You moved out.

                CAT
Oh, you wanna bring that up! So that's what's eatin' ya'! Yeah, I moved out. You know why I left. You ought-a know...you was right there.

            (SPANKY clams up again.)

                CAT
I said you was right there...I'm talking to you, Spanky...

                SPANKY
I'm listening to ya'.

                CAT
How the hell do I know you listening? The day I left, I called all four-a you boys 'round the table and told y'all why I was leaving. Did you listen to me then? Did you hear me then, Spanky?

SPANKY
You shouldn't-a left.

CAT
Shouldn't'a left? Ain't this a bitch! Didn't you hear me say your mama told me she didn't want me no mo,' didn't need me no mo'? After I'd done bought and paid for the house and y'all was up some size, she told me I could stay there if I rented one-a the rooms...if I paid rent in my own house! Like I was some boarder! And you thought I should-a stayed and took that!

(SPANKY lets a beat pass.)

SPANKY
I can see that part was wrong, but...

CAT
But what? But what, Spanky?!

SPANKY
I just think you either should-a stayed or took us with you.

CAT
The day your mama told me to leave, she said, "My sons can take care-a me from now on." If I'd'a took y'all with me, who was gonna take care'a her? She hadn't never worked a day in her life...didn't know nothing but taking care-a y'all.

Coming To The Mercy Seat

(A beat. CAT's frustration grows.)

CAT

Should'a took y'all with me! Why didn't y'all leave with me? You was big enough to say who you wanted to go with.

SPANKY

I wanted to go with you.

CAT

What is this you telling me now, Spanky!? How was I supposed to know any'a y'all wanted to go with me, the way y'all was acting? Y'all would be in the living room watching T.V. 'Soon as I come in and start watching with y'all, all of you would git up and go in your room. Then soon as I turn if off and leave, y'all would come back in and start watching it...when I come back, y'all leave again. You think that didn't hurt me?! You think I didn't have no feelings?

(SPANKY squirms, guilty.)

CAT

Wanted to go with me! If just *one'a* y'all had'a said that, my life would'a been different these past twenty years. You think I liked living like a grasshopper? Christmas, Easter, Thanksgiving come and not a letter or a card! People thought I didn't have no family! And what about Father's Day? How you think I felt seeing boys going to church with they red flowers on, and me wondering if y'all was wearing red flowers of if you considered me dead? Then when you git on your ass, you show up at my door!

SPANKY
I know we was wrong...I wanna make it up to you...

CAT
You can't make up nothing to me! Just get your own life together, 'cause you don't know how it hurt me to see you like this. You was the best son I had...always had you a little something to do, even if it wasn't nothing but taking people's trash out. People would say, "Yonder go Cat's boy! He gonna make something out'a his'self!" I kept my chest stuck out! Now look at you!

SPANKY
I just got a little turned around, pop...that's all. I see people out at the hospital: teachers, judges, even doctors...you be surprised, they fall, too.

CAT
Spanky, what do you want from me? I tried to be the best father I could be to y'all. Sometime I think God is punishing me for something! I see other mens...it's a man at church that's got five sons and all of 'em done made something out'a they'selves...!

SPANKY
I bet their fathers called them by their names and gave them affection when they was growing up.

Coming To The Mercy Seat

CAT
What?

SPANKY
What's my name, pop?

CAT
Your name?

SPANKY
What's my name?

CAT
I named you Curtis. If you talking 'bout that Spanky-shit, go blame your mama for that...that's her shit.

SPANKY
What about the affection, pop?

CAT
Affection?

SPANKY
You heard me. You never gave us no affection, and I ain't going nowhere 'til I get mine!

CAT
Hell, ain't no father never gave me no affection, and it didn't stop me from being a man!

SPANKY
You never wanted no love and affection from your father? I wanna hear you say to my face that you never wanted your father's love and affection.

CAT
I ain't had no time to sit on my ass pining for what I didn't git from my father! I had to cut cane and haul wood from the time I was four years old! I didn't even know who my father was 'til I was almost a grown man! Affection! If that's all you got to squawk about, you ain't got no case! You had a father right there in the house with you that kept a roof over your head and food on the table all during your boyhood years. You can't point to n'ary day that you went hungry or n'eked, 'cause I did what a man was supposed to do...!

SPANKY
Pop, if it was just me, I would say you was right, but look at Junior, and look at Ron...

CAT
Yeah, look at 'em! Naw, ain't none of 'em worth a good'damn, but they ain't showed up at my door blaming me for nothing, and if they got that much pride about 'em, they got *some* kind'a manhood, and that's more than I can say for you!

> (SPANKY is stung to the quick. A whole beat passes, and then SPANKY resigns himself.)

Coming To The Mercy Seat

          SPANKY
All right, pop. You win. You asked me to leave, so I'll leave.

          (SPANKY heads out...and then CAT adjusts his attitude.)

          CAT
Spanky...Curtis...you almost forty years old, son! I can't feed and suckle you like you some baby! You gotta give me some kind-a sign...!

          SPANKY
Pop, I lost something of myself...I just wanna stay here 'til I get back on track. The psychiatrist gonna give me a disability letter...

          CAT
Psychiatrist! Curtis, you been all cross the water! Uncle Sam didn't think you was crazy! The peoples out at that hospital all say you the best they ever had at that medical stuff...'say you know it better than some'a them doctors. *They* don't think you crazy!

          SPANKY
They working on getting me back out there.

          CAT
If you don't quit that drinking, Curtis...if you keep messing up...!

SPANKY
I'm gonna quit, pop...I'm declaring it. Remember, whenever I said *I declare*, I would always be telling the truth?

> (A beat.)

CAT
All I want you to do if you gonna stay here is open your mouth and talk to me when I say something to you. Half the time, I don't even know if you hear me talking to you.

SPANKY
I be hearing you.

CAT
You gotta make me know it, son. I know it's some things I didn't learn how to do as a father, but I can't change the past. Maybe if you come go to church with me. All y'all used to go with me.

SPANKY
Yes'sir. I'm gonna go to church with you.

> (A beat. Both men feel awkward in the silence.
>
> CAT takes a key from his pocket.)

CAT
Git this key cut...

Coming To The Mercy Seat

                    SPANKY
Yes-sir.

                    CAT
And put it on a ring or something this time.

                    SPANKY
Yes-sir.

                    CAT
I want you to know something, 'cause I guess you don't remember it...but when y'all was boys, y'all used to run meet me at the bus line when I got off from work and jump all up in my arms and hug my neck. I'd hug y'all tight...real tight...'cause I was proud, see? I was proud!

                    SPANKY
Yes'sir. It's just that...I can't remember what that felt like, daddy.

                    After a beat, father and son overcome their hesitation and embrace.

                    Then we hear CURTIS's quiet sobbing.)

END

J.e Franklin

It is possible to belong to two men
One who creates you
And one who raises you

One who stands by
While the other gives you all of his love,
Attention and devotion.

One who feeds you and disciplines you
While the other dictates.
Yes, it is possible to be

Two mens'es daughter.

N'zinga

Coming To The Mercy Seat

TWO MENS'ES DAUGHTER

J.e Franklin

CHARACTERS IN ORDER OF APPEARANCE

Aunt Goldie, 65 plus, light enough to pass

ADDIE - 18 - 20

Coming To The Mercy Seat

> GOLDIE is an invalid. She is dipping snuff when the action begins.
>
> When she hears someone coming, she is about to attack with the first thing she gets her hands on.

GOLDIE
Now, who's that coming in here?!

ADDIE
Don't shoot, Aunt Goldie, it's me-Addie!

GOLDIE
Don't tell me they done sent *you* over here, too!

ADDIE
No-mam, Aunt Goldie, ain't *no*body sent *me*! I'm on *your* side!

GOLDIE
The next one come over here dev'lin me 'bout going to some funeral, I'm gonna throw something at 'em and try my best to kill 'em!

ADDIE
Then there'll be *two* funerals, huh, Aunt Goldie?!

GOLDIE
H'it shore will be!

ADDIE
I told 'em they better leave you alone! But they say if you

don't go to that funeral, you knocking them out-a their part-a that money.

GOLDIE
Hit's a *part*, all right! I bet it ain't nothing but chicken-feed!

ADDIE
Aunt Goldie, you know what? That Ol' Avril Morrow came by the house.

GOLDIE
That skunk! I figured he'd show up soon's he smelt money! He know bettern to come here!

ADDIE
He told Aunt Tootie and Uncle Cecil David that they was left $10,000 a'piece, Aunt Goldie!

GOLDIE
I bet'cha he didn't tell how much *he* was left!

ADDIE
He didn't say how much *you* was left, either, but I got the feeling you was left more than anybody 'cause every time your name was mentioned, he'd get that hate-look in his eyes!

GOLDIE
Damn his eyes and their'n, too! Let 'em bury every cent-a that dev'lish money with they so-called daddy to keep him in cigars down in hell!

ADDIE
They say even if their part ain't but ten dollars, if their

Coming To The Mercy Seat

daddy left it to 'em, they want it. They real mad at you, Aunt Goldie!

GOLDIE
You ever knowed your auntie to care 'bout somebody being mad at her?

AUNT
N'ome!

GOLDIE
Well, then! Let 'em get mad and sad and scratch up they ass til they get glad! They daddy! Which one of 'em is over there calling him *daddy*? I 'members when they called him a ol' low'down peckerwood and any other name they could think of, but they was to chicken-shit to say it to his face, so they put me up to it!

ADDIE
When I was little, I used to hear y'awl call him names. That's why you could-a knocked me over with a feather just now when Aunt Tootie and Uncle Cecil David told me that Old Man Morrow was y'awl's daddy!

GOLDIE
What *y'awl*? He wasn't no daddy-a mines! The onliest daddy I ever recognized was <u>Mister</u> Emmanuel Henry Randall! And Daddy Randall was the onliest daddy they ever knowed, too! Would you call some white grasshopper *daddy* just 'cause he gave you a few nickels ever'now and then...just cause you *heard* he was your daddy?

ADDIE
N'ome.

J.e Franklin

GOLDIE
'Cause you got plenty sense! Them fools over there ain't got none!

ADDIE
Did you tell 'em they could put your name on that obituary, Aunt Goldie?

GOLDIE
'Say they puttin' my name on the 'bituary?! My name done already 'peared on a 'bituary as Daddy Randall's daughter! How I'm gonna be *two* mens'es daughter!

ADDIE
I don't reckon you can be, unless you got a holy-ghost daddy!

GOLDIE
If they don't get my name off that dev'lish 'bituary, I'll crawl over there some kind-a way and roll over 'em like The Rock-a Ages!

ADDIE
I heard a certain person on the phone telling somebody Old Man Morrow is survived by five offspring. They named Avril and Miss Pam by the white lady....that's two right there!

GOLDIE
H'it was old Tootie, wasn't it?

ADDIE
I ain't calling no name, Aunt Goldie!

Coming To The Mercy Seat

GOLDIE
You ain't got to tell me...I know she the ring'tail leader! I done told that heiffer to keep my name out-a her dev'lish mouth!

ADDIE
I ain't saying she called your name, Aunt Goldie, but where do *five* come from if she wasn't counting you, Uncle Cecil David, and herself?

GOLDIE
Herself, huh? So it *was* her?! Old ass-licker!

(ADDIE realizes her error too late.)

ADDIE
Uhhh...

GOLDIE
I swear on my dead mama's grave, I'll show up at that church house, all right, but not for the reason they want! If God give me the strength, I'll rise up out'a this chair like Lazarus and give a testimony'll make they so-called daddy come up out that casket and curse the day he ever laid eyes on my dark mother!

ADDIE
I know you don't play, Aunt Goldie! I remember that Sunday Rev. Hill come preaching to everybody about fornicating, and you got up and told the whole congregation you saw him sneaking out-a the back door of Sister Leach's house.

GOLDIE
You 'member that!?

J.e Franklin

ADDIE
Yes-mam...I was little but I remember it!

GOLDIE
I'm too old a cat to be called a kitten! That's why auntie don't go to none-a these churches like she used to...they filled with 'publicans and hypocrites! I ain't never set foot inside no white church house, but this is one time I'll set foot in one! If they don't take my name off that dev'lish 'bituary, you gonna hear auntie preach a sermon they won't never forget!

ADDIE
If I could pass for white like you and Aunt Tootie and Uncle Cecil David, I would stand by your side while you preached it, but they might not even let me in the door!

AUNT GOLDIE
I ain't never tried to pass for white, me. Tootie n'em walk in a white place just as big and bold and have people thinking they white! I don't wanna go nowhere all my peoples can't go! I tells 'em in a minute, I'm Colored and proud of it!

ADDIE
I'm surprised Old Man Morrow would want y'awl at his funeral...be more likely he'd try to hide the fact he had outside children, especially by a Colored woman!

AUNT GOLDIE
Hide it from who? Ha!

ADDIE
Did his wife know?!

Coming To The Mercy Seat

AUNT GOLDIE
Did she! I wish I had a nickel for every white woman what know her husband is foolin' with Colored womens! I'd be so rich, I wouldn't need nobody's money! He made that dev'lish will out that'a-way to get back at her for something! And still trying to make me bow down to him and figure that mess he got in his will gonna make me do it. Well, he got another thought coming!

ADDIE
Aunt Goldie, you remember that big case years ago where some white man in Louisiana left a whole pile of money? His will said the same thing Old Man Morrow's will is saying: that his white children couldn't get none of the money unless his Colored children could come to his funeral.

AUNT GOLDIE
So one white monkey done copied off another white monkey! Monkey see, monkey do! That was him, all right!

ADDIE
He should'a known better than to try to tempt you with money, 'cause you ain't never cared nothing for no money! Every since I was little, if you had it, we had it. You'll give a person the shirt off your back!

GOLDIE
I 'member one time I gave this woman my last pair good drawers 'cause the rubber in hers had popped. I didn't care, honey! We all comes in this world n'eked. We sees people with clothes on when they gets funeralized, but I heard tell they digs them graves up after everybody leave

and takes even them few rags off they behind!

ADDIE
I guess Old Man Morrow didn't figure you'd stay away from that funeral and keep the others from getting their money.

AUNT GOLDIE
What I wanna put myself out for them for? They ain't never did nothing for me.

ADDIE
Uncle Cecil David ain't gonna do nothing but gamble his away, and all of Aunt Tootie's is going downtown to the bail-bondsman to get Sonny Jr. out-a jail for something he ain't had no business doing. Theirs'll be gone in a week.

AUNT GOLDIE
Sooner than that, honey. Then they'll be over here begging me for whatever I had left.

ADDIE
And you'd give it to 'em little by little until it was all gone...'cause you just good'hearted like that, Aunt Goldie. You good as gold! That's why I'd do anything for you!

GOLDIE
Aunt Goldie shore do love you honey. You the onliest one understand!

ADDIE
At first I thought you should go to Old Man Morrow's funeral, but I'm glad you ain't going 'cause now Ol' Avril Morrow's gonna get payback for what he did to me last week.

Coming To The Mercy Seat

GOLDIE
What'd he do?

ADDIE
I was scrubbing floors in the cafeteria, and he got a cupfull-a dirt and threw it on the floor, then said, "Clean it up, buckwheat," and had everybody laughing at me.

GOLDIE
Why, that low'down, dirty scound'! He just mean to that! Why'n you come tell auntie?

ADDIE
'Cause you always say *every dog'll have his day, and a good dog'll have two days.* I just asked my supervisor to let me clean inside the dorms where I can't be seen in the open.

GOLDIE
Next time you see him, ask him ain't he the one shit in his britches when his dev'lish daddy brought him out here one time...wouldn't car'ry him home to his own mammy to clean...naw, wanted my mama to do it!

ADDIE
Did Grandma Randall clean him, Aunt Goldie?

GOLDIE
Mama was just good-hearted like that! Daddy Randall thought I took after her, but I knew I wasn't fit to eat her doo-doo! When people did mama wrong, she'd forgive 'em...me, I'd lay in wait for 'em for years, killing 'em in my heart long after they'd done forgot about it. Then I'd make 'em sorry they ever crossed me!

ADDIE
One day I'll be a student out at the University just like Ol' Avril. I hope and pray he'll still be going there by the time I save enough money to go. Then I'll show him something! If I had the money I'd enroll now. Miss Kemp's daughter goes to the nursing school, and Sister William's nephew is studying engineering out there...

GOLDIE
I believes Rev. Hill did say something about 'em studying out there. Bless their hearts!

ADDIE
I would study the law...but that costs so much more than the other courses... there're so many books to buy!

(A beat.)

GOLDIE
Bless your heart! Wanna study the law!

ADDIE
Aunt Goldie...has anybody in our family ever gone to college?

GOLDIE
None that I knows of. One time, mama tried to get me to go to some missionary college, but honey, I ain't wanna be no nun! They said I'd have to give up my snuff! Shoot, bad enough I'd have to give up my chuchie!

ADDIE
I'd give up almost anything to go to college, but I wouldn't want you giving up your pride and going to no ol' funeral just so I could go, Aunt Goldie. I'll find a way.

Coming To The Mercy Seat

(A beat.)

GOLDIE
What they charge for something like that?

ADDIE
Well...for state residents, it costs four thousand dollars. I would study hard, Aunt Goldie, and make you proud of me....make the whole family proud!

GOLDIE
It would make you-know-who turn over in his grave! He didn't mind doing coitus with Colored women, and now want us crying over his casket, but just say white and Colored settin' in a school'room together and he'd have a 'niptian'fit!

ADDIE
From what I heard about him, though, Aunt Goldie—and I didn't hear much--- it seems like he respected the ones who stood up for their rights. Seems like he shore respected you!

(A beat, as GOLDIE reflects.)

GOLDIE
Humph! How they plan on getting to that thing?

ADDIE
Avril Morrow said a car is being sent to pick everybody up.

GOLDIE
No doubt h'it's gonna be some old piecy trap they got off

the junkyard.

ADDIE
N'ome. Aunt Tootie say it's gonna be a brand new Cadillac.

GOLDIE
Humph! No doubt they gonna put us at the back-a the whole funeral train.

ADDIE
N'ome. Old Man Morrow wants the car with you and Aunt Tootie and Uncle Cecil David right behind the hearst.

GOLDIE
Think I'm gonna feel something for him in his death that I didn't feel in his life! Humph!

ADDIE
I always wanted to ask you why you hated him so, but I was scared to. I figured he must-a done something!

GOLDIE
All of 'em should-a hated him, the way he treated Daddy Randall, never puttin' no handle on his name, coming out here like he owned my mama! Like he had a right to her!

>(GOLDIE's anger leaves ADDIE unsure of how to respond. This is a new GOLDIE she is seeing. Finally, GOLDIE recovers.)

GOLDIE
Mama wasn't nothing but a kid when she went to work for him. She said everywhere she turned, there he was. Even

Coming To The Mercy Seat

after Daddy Randall married her, he kept coming around. Ain't many Colored men wants a Colored woman got white men's chill'un, but Daddy Randall loved us just like we was his'n. Ol' Morrow wanted to get even, cheated him out'a some money, mad cause he married mama. What could a Colored man do back then? He didn't have no rights a white man was bound to respect. I hadn't even quit peeing-the-bed yet the first time I cussed him. I didn't know what I was saying...just repeating what the grown-folks said. He told mama to beat me, but she wouldn't. That let me believe I could keep it up...and I did it, even after he told me he was my daddy. I told him, "You might be the one sired me, but you ain't my daddy. If I pass on the road and see you laying in a gully bleeding to death, I'll pass on by like I don't even know you and let you die!" Me being the baby, I could get away with anything. Everybody was scared he was gonna sic the Cu-Kluk-Klan on me, but he didn't. I didn't care. Something had a holt'a me! Mama would say---real quiet— "Don't do evil for evil, baby. When somebody do you evil, do 'em good." But I knowed her heart—or thought I did—'til one day she told me I had ways just like him. I'm 'shamed to even repeat what I said to my mama! I know I hurt her to her heart, 'cause she just left me to God! When your mama leave you to God, she's through with you forever! 'Cause the Bible tell you not to cuss your mama—or your daddy—or your lamp be put out in everlasting darkness! That's why I stays in this room...guess I'm just waiting for the lamp to go out!

ADDIE
I used to wonder what inspired Langston Hughes to write that poem he wrote about a story just like this one.

GOLDIE
What poem was that?

J.e Franklin

ADDIE
The one we had to learn in high school, called *Cross*, that went:

> *My old man was a white old man*
> *And my old mama was black.*
> *If ever I cursed my white old man,*
> *I take my curses back.*

> **(At some point in the poem, GOLDIE joins in. That's when ADDIE stops and listens, surprised that GOLDIE knows it.)**

GOLDIE
If ever I cursed my black old mother
And wished her soul in hell,
I'm sorry for that evil wish
And now I wish them well.

> **(GOLDIE begins to weep, and ADDIE comforts her, enfolding her lovingly.)**

ADDIE
Aw, Aunt Goldie...they forgive you! Both of them...I know they do, Aunt Goldie! I know they forgive you!

END

Coming To The Mercy Seat

You can't judge me.
That's not your job.
Was he here
When I was sick?

Did he cook for me, clean for me?
Was it him I traveled with
Took long walks with?
Cried with?

Did my kids come
When I needed them?
But him. He saw my plight, my pain
And he sent me someone.

Someone who does all those things
And loves me.
So, yes, sista, I'm shacking up
Shacking up gray...

But by His design.

N'zinga

J.e Franklin

SHACKING UP GREY

Coming To The Mercy Seat

CHARACTERS IN ORDER OF APPEARANCE

LORRAINE - 65 - 70

MONICA - 60 - 65

J.e Franklin

LORRAINE is packing her suitcase when her sister MONICA enters.

MONICA
Lorraine, what do you call yourself doing?

LORRAINE
I'm going to a hotel until my plane leaves.

MONICA
You're just being silly.

LORRAINE
Call me all the names you want. You wasn't raised like this, and if papa and mama could see you now, they'd turn over in their graves!

MONICA
Let 'em turn! I've earned the right to do anything I feel like doing as long as I'm not hurting nobody.

LORRAINE
You ain't got no right to involve me in it. I was looking forward to a few days of rest, and I come here and find out you shacked up with some man! I know people are talking!

MONICA
Let 'em talk! They don't come over here and hold my hand when I'm hurting.

LORRAINE
Well, what about me? If you don't care about *your* reputation, what about mine? People probably think every

Coming To The Mercy Seat

woman in the family shacks up common-law! No wonder you didn't want me talking to nobody around here.

MONICA
'Cause I knew you'd act like this if you found out...you're so judgmental!

LORRAINE
I ain't judging you half as much as The Good Judge up on high! You ain't gonna spot my garment before The Lord!

MONICA
Spot your garment! I don't even believe in that mess no more!

LORRAINE
What is this you saying?! You don't believe in *God* no more?!

MONICA
I believe there's a God...I just don't believe in all that other stuff.

LORRAINE
All what other stuff?!

MONICA
If there *is* a God...

LORRAINE
If?! You never would-a reached old-age except for his Grace! Now you're here blaspheming like some Doubting Thomas! Lord, help me get out-a here 'fore you throw some thunder at this house and strike it down!

MONICA
You didn't let me finish, Lorraine. I was gonna say if God sees and knows all, then He must know what a double yoke it is to be old and Black in this land. You must know what that's like, too.

LORRAINE
Shore, I know! I feel that yoke from time to time, but I ain't lost my religion. I still believe in that old time religion, back in the day when a girl or woman was made to stand up before the congregation and ask forgiveness for going wrong!

MONICA
Forgiveness for what?! Did I steal something? Did I bear false witness against my neighbor? Who did I murder?

LORRAINE
You are fornicating!

MONICA
Don't come here preaching to me! Now, I'm just as stout as you are stiff! My pastor knows about my relationship with Gil and he has given us his blessings.

LORRAINE
Yeah, I guess he would, at that old so-called church with that old funny-sounding music and the women wearing britches to the service! These churches now-a'days is just done gone to the devil, and the preachers is kicking up more ruckus than the sinners and publicans they supposed to be saving! I knew the Holy Spirit wasn't in that den you took me to, 'cause the church bells did better work than the sermon.

MONICA
Do you want me to go to a old folks home, Lorraine?

Coming To The Mercy Seat

LORRAINE
Now, why would you ask a foolish question like that?

MONICA
Then what do you want me to do? Most of my friends are dead and gone, and half of 'em had been dead two or three days before somebody found them. I don't wanna die that way. I feel lonely and powerless when I'm by myself. I need companionship.

LORRAINE
How come he don't wanna marry you?

MONICA
Marry? For what?! So we can have children?

LORRAINE
People our age don't get married? Oh, but that would be too much like right!

MONICA
Right ain't got nothing to do with it. You know what we'd have to go through to keep Uncle Sam from messing with my social security and Gil's pension...!

LORRAINE
Oh, a pension! I *figured* he was old enough to be drawing one! He probably got so many things wrong with him, you'll end up running back and forth to the hospital with him!

MONICA
So what? He ran back and forth with me. After my operation, I couldn't even lift my arms to wash myself! He picked me up, put me in that tub and bathed me down,

grocery shopped, cooked, cleaned, anything I needed him to do! I didn't have nobody else to do it.

LORRAINE

You got three children.

MONICA

Shoot! Just as well to have none! I don't hear from T-Boy 'til he want something. Arlene's out in Detroit living the life of Reilly. Bud's right here in town, but do you think he comes to check on me to see if I'm dead or alive?

LORRAINE

He probably don't come 'cause he know what he gonna find.

MONICA

I couldn't turn to my children even *before* Gil came here to live.

LORRAINE

I can turn to my children! They can come to my house *anytime* 'cause they know they ain't gonna catch some man tipping out-a my bedroom.

MONICA

My children don't run my life.

LORRAINE

I don't see but one bed. You gonna tell me he sleep on the couch?

MONICA

No, I'm not gonna tell you that lie.

Coming To The Mercy Seat

LORRAINE
Well, that's a switch! So you sleep in the same bed. For God-sake, what do y'all do?!

MONICA
Lorraine, what do you think we do?

LORRAINE
Well! I do declare!

MONICA
Gil might not have much pep in his step, but he got it where it counts!

LORRAINE
How you talk! You gonna give up a home on high for something down here on this wicked earth that's got one foot in the grave and look like he's on his way to glory?!

MONICA
This is the happiest I've been in all my years. Gil is taking me places...Africa, India, Paris...places I always wanted to see. He got flying money and we gonna fly! I'm getting me some happiness these few years I got left. I shore didn't know none when Dennis was alive! He got to be touchy and selfish, always acting important and trying to give me advice, yet he couldn't get his own life together. Gil is considerate and affectionate. He admires and cherishes me! If God begrudge a little happiness to two people who ain't did nothing to Him, then He ain't all He's trumped up to be! And what about you, Lorraine? When have *you* been happy? Your marriage wasn't peaches and cream, either.

LORRAINE
No, it wasn't peaches and cream, but I got married for better

or worse. It was a woman's duty to stay with her husband til death do us part. I took a lot off Rufus. Running out with other women, gambling and staying out late, but he kept food on the table, and I did what I could with the Lord's help. And since Rufus died, ain't no man seen under my clothes!

MONICA

You skin your cat and I'll skin mine.

LORRAINE

I'm gonna pray for you...you don't know what you're doing! We supposed to give that stuff up at our age and look forward to heaven!

MONICA

When did you get to be so self-righteous?! When we were girls, you was *Miss Sweet Lorraine...*

LORRAINE

That's all in the past. I been born again! I'm getting ready for my heavenly home now, and my heart gets light when I think of how it won't be long before I go there!

MONICA

Born again! You need to cut this mess out, Lorraine! And you better be careful how you paint God! The way you talk, God don't sound no different from the devil! That's blasphemy! God knows we out-live our Black men by 18 years! What kind of God would want us to be lonely for 18 years?! Loneliness is a disease! God didn't tell us we had to go to the senior citizen center and dance with another woman 'cause all our men are dead. I believe you scared me and Gil's relationship is gonna rub off on you!

Coming To The Mercy Seat

LORRAINE
(Getting defensive)
Rub off on me?! Ain't nothing rubbing off on me! I'm just concerned about you! If Gil dies, his whole family is coming in here. I know a woman that happened to...the man's people got everything. People said it was a shame they didn't get married...the woman could-a been well off. She had to bury the man all by herself...his people didn't give her nothing on that funeral!

MONICA
If Gil's people want this junk, they can have it! He ain't worried about when he die, so why should I? We *living* now! We got tickets to the theater, and to dinner, then we going for a drive in the car! I don't have to walk these streets by myself night *or* day! And what about you, Lorraine? Your children might come to see you, but where were they the night you was putting your key in the door and you got dragged off the porch, down the steps, all out in the middle of the streets trying to hold onto your pocketbook? If the strap hadn't broke, you could-a been dragged to death behind that car they sped off in!

(LORRAINE begins to stammer.)

LORRAINE
Well...the children would-a been there for me. They call...from time to time.

MONICA
To beg you for something.

LORRAINE
I know my children love me...

(LORRAINE's lips begin to quiver.)

MONICA
But do they love you the way you want 'em to love you? Do they love and do for you the way you did for them when they couldn't do for themselves?

(LORRAINE'S mood has changed now.)

MONICA
These children think as long as they buy a bag-a groceries and come put it in the refrigerator, I don't need nothing else, but I do.

(A beat)

MONICA
You still got them old plastic flowers they gave you three years ago for Mother's Day?

LORRAINE
Now, why did you have to bring that up? You just wanna hurt me!

MONICA
Why would I wanna hurt you?

LORRAINE
I don't know why!

MONICA
I know we both got good children..but they don't know what a mother mean. You ruin your health worrying over 'em all their life, then they abandon you!

Coming To The Mercy Seat

(MONICA suddenly notices LORRAINE state.)

MONICA
Oh, Lorraine...I didn't mean to...!

LORRAINE
Sometime I feel so heartsick!

MONICA
Oh, don't cry! I never could stand to see you cry. Pull yourself together now...it's gonna be all right.

(The two sisters weep and comfort each other.)

THE END

J.e Franklin

He never kicked like the others,
Never moved like the others.
With him, she knew
Something just wasn't right.

How do you love a child so hard to love,
Hard to teach,
Hard to understand?
But after all of that—

When you've given all of your love,
Been the best teacher
And gave all of your patience—
How do you put that child away?

How do you put Pippy away—?

                                        N'zinga

Coming To The Mercy Seat

PUTTIN' PIPPY AWAY

J.e Franklin

CHARACTERS IN ORDER OF APPEARANCE

Emma, 65 plus

Ethyl, 40

Pippy, 30

Coming To The Mercy Seat

>PIPPY, ETHYL's late baby, is a mentally-challenged adult.
>
>When the play opens, he is seated on the floor near ETHYL and is trying to make a yo-yo behave.
>
>EMMA enters, in a take-charge frame of mind.

EMMA
Mama, what are you doing out-a bed!

ETHYL
I was trying to phone you just now...

EMMA
Phone me for what? I told you what time I'd be here. Are Pippy's things ready?

ETHYL
I was trying to catch you before you left the house to tell you don't come.

EMMA
Don't come? Mama don't start this again!

ETHYL
I have a right to change my mind...

EMMA
Mama, everything has been arranged...his bed is ready...you signed the papers!

ETHYL
You the one signed 'em...all I did was put my X on 'em.

EMMA
Mama, you knew what you were signing. I read every line of those papers to you. This is the third time you've pulled this. Those people are gonna think we're playing some kind-a game.

ETHYL
Well, I don't wanna do it.

EMMA
You said you would let me handle things.

ETHYL
I tried to put it in the hands-a Jesus, but I feel like Judas in my heart.

EMMA
I'm the one taking him there, so will you let me bear the burden of the guilty, if there is any? If this had been done thirty years ago, me and Willie might-a had some kind-a childhood. That's why half the time we don't know where he is.

ETHYL
I know you both is 'shamed-a your brother.

Coming To The Mercy Seat

EMMA
It ain't the idea of being ashamed...I didn't come here to talk about that, mama. I just wanna get it clear about Pippy.

ETHYL
It's already clear...he ain't going.

EMMA
Then who's gonna look after him when I'm at work, mama? Name the person?

ETHYL
God's gonna send somebody.

EMMA
Is God gonna pay 'em? People wanna get paid, and that little check Pippy get ain't nothing. If we don't take this spot now, it may be months before another one opens up...then he'll have to go up to Rusk.

ETHYL
No! I don't want him up there! They gonna be mistreating him.

EMMA
I'm doing all I can to keep him from going to Rusk, but you fighting me, mama, and this is wearing me out.

ETHYL
Suppose them doctors is wrong? They ain't right about everything...they told me you was a tumor.

EMMA
Mama, why did you have me call the lawyer last week to get everything straight with the house?

(A beat. ETHYL does not dare to answer this.)

ETHYL

Well...

EMMA

You may as well go'on say it. You don't know how long those treatments are gonna last and you don't know what the outcome is gonna be.

ETHYL

This may sound harsh, but I find myself wishing God would take him first so I can lay my head down in peace.

EMMA

I don't think it sound harsh. And if you ask me, trying to take care-a Pippy all these years is what ruined your health. You're tired, mama!

ETHYL

This child ain't ruined my health...if anybody ruined it, it was me having to run back and forth to lawyers and bail bondsmen to get that other brother-a yours out jail for something he ain't had no business doing. This baby never gave me no kind-a trouble. He never harmed nobody, never stole nothing, never lied or hated nobody...

EMMA

Well, mama, Pippy ain't got sense enough to do none-a that.

ETHYL

Oh, is that what it take to do evil? Sense? There's all kind-a sense, you know. Even a horse got horse-sense. I'm glad this

Coming To The Mercy Seat

baby ain't got the kind-a sense that make him lie and steal and kill and hate, but he shore got *some* kind-a sense. Just to show you, the other night, I heard somebody moving around. I got up and he was emptying the wastebaskets at 2 o'clock in the morning 'cause he forgot to take that trash out before he went to sleep. And when one-a his little friends died at his school, he was sad for weeks. He got sense you don't understand...

EMMA
Mama, I don't wanna war with you. I love Pippy and I'll miss him traipsing up behind me like a little puppy'dog. Even when we were kids and you'd bring him over to the school when you came to see about us...me and Willie got teased about him, but still we loved him.

ETHYL
Everybody get teased about *something*. Look at how they teased Jesus and made him wear a crown-a thorns...nailed him to a tree like a crow! But he got a home on high now, ain't he? I told all you chil'ren not to pay no'tention to the words of fools.

EMMA
We tried to ignore 'em when we could, but it was just too many fools...even some of the teachers. If we got a word or a problem wrong, seemed like them big red marks they'd put on our paper was bigger than the marks they'd put on the other children's paper.

ETHYL
I tried with the help of the Lord to protect y'awl as much as I could.

EMMA
I know you did, mama. And I'm sorry you never got the grandchildren you always wished for, but me and Willie made a pact.

ETHYL
What pact? Pact about what?

EMMA
A pact not to bring no Pippy into the world.

ETHYL
Why, you fools, you! You didn't have to do that! Pippy is just marked! He was marked with the grief touching before he was even thought of!

EMMA
Oh, mama, please! I don't even believe in that old plantation hoo'doo talk!

ETHYL
Well, I believes it! I was told by a old conjure woman when I was a girl, that one-a my chil'ren would be a dry'birth baby. I knew Pippy was the one 'cause he felt different...he didn't kick like you and Willie. I told them doctors he was the one, and they didn't believe me, neither. When I knew I was carrying him, there was times—and I know this sound cold—there was times I was tempted to take something. I hope God forgive me for having them ugly thoughts.

EMMA
It don't sound cold to me. Willie wanted to put him downtown with a cup. And as for daddy, you heard how *he* denied Pippy. He accused Uncle Jimmy of being his daddy.

Coming To The Mercy Seat

ETHYL
I never paid no attention to your daddy's fool talk. Didn't Peter deny Jesus three times?

EMMA
Daddy wanted to have him put to sleep.

ETHYL
Abraham wanted to sacrifice his son, too, but God wouldn't let him. You see who got put to sleep first.

EMMA
Just the same, it's times like these I wish daddy was alive.

ETHYL
I don't. He'd be leading the pack to put this baby away...po'little thing!

EMMA
Mama, ain't nobody raring to put Pippy away. Didn't we take our time and look at different places. You said you had a good feeling about this one. It's clean, the staff is warm and caring, there's plenty of activities and trips. Pippy make friends easy.

ETHYL
Nobody asked him if he wanna go there. If he knew he was leaving me, maybe for good, he'd show you something! 'Cause even hogs know! When they 'bout to go to the slaughterhouse, they squeal and run and carry on! Pippy...come here to mama, honey...

(PIPPY obeys.)

ETHYL
Do you believe mama love you? See there? Look at how he smile at me? You might not see your po'old mama no more in this life. Now look at how sad he look after I say that. I told you he got sense.

EMMA
Mama, I know he got sense. He understand when I play coon-can with him...and he understand going for a ride. Pippy...I'm going for a ride in the car-car...wanna go for a ride?

(PIPPY smiles and is about
to follow EMMA, but ETHYL
holds him back.)

ETHYL
Don't deceive him like that. She ain't going for no ride, baby...she fixing to put you away!

(PIPPY grows alarmed and
clings to his mother.)

EMMA
Mama, don't do this...why don't you cut this out?

ETHYL
He don't wanna go!

EMMA
So ask him if he rather go up to Rusk! I'll take him to whichever one he wants to go to. He going to *one* of 'em, over your dead body or your live one, or you can take him to the grave with you! 'Cause I'm tired...!

Coming To The Mercy Seat

(ETHYL clutches her heart.)

EMMA
Now, see there...! Look at what you're bringing on! Why didn't you tell me you was gonna act like this before I took off from work? Think about what this is doing to me. You see Willie ain't here to help...all this mess getting dumped on me. It's not fair, mama...I gotta live my life, too. Just tell me what you want me to do!

(ETHYL tries to catch her breath.)

ETHYL
I don't see why I can't go with y'awl.

EMMA
Because the doctor said...he advised you not to travel...

ETHYL
I don't care if it kills me.

EMMA
Not in my car, mama....I mean...ain't it enough that I'd have my hands full with Pippy?

(A beat)

ETHYL
Will you promise you'll go visit him as often as you can?

EMMA
Mama, you don't have to ask me that...you know I'll go visit my little brother.

J.e Franklin

ETHYL
Don't let 'em mistreat him.

EMMA
I'll be on the lookout. If I see any signs of abuse, I'll be all over 'em like white on rice!

ETHYL
Pippy...you 'member them times mama whipped you? Will you forgive mama?

EMMA
Mama, you know he don't hold no malice in his heart.

(ETHYL holds PIPPY to her, and
EMMA gently pries him loose.)

EMMA
Mama, let him go...he'll be all right.

ETHYL
Go with Emma now...

(ETHYL slowly releases him.)

EMMA
Come on, Pip. We gotta go, buddy. Tell mother'dear you gotta go drive the car'car. Wave bye-bye to mother'dear.

(EMMA pantomimes driving.
PIPPY overcomes his hesitation
and follows innocently.)

EMMA
Tell mother'dear you'll see her later. Say, "I'll see ya' later,

Coming To The Mercy Seat

alligator."

>(As he is being led out, he squeals, glancing back at ETHYL for a sign. But she restrains herself....and then, after she is alone, she breaks into sobs.)

ETHYL

My po' little baby! Lord, have mercy on my po' little baby!

END

J.e Franklin

You s'pozed to be his daddy.
No matter what he does
What he says.
Let a child act like a child.

Let a man be a man.
Let him humble himself to you.
Let him be your son.
Please let me see my son.

You s'pozed to be his daddy.

N'zinga

S'POZED-TO-BE DADDY

CHARACTERS IN ORDER OF APPEARANCE

Gideon, 65 plus

Gussie Lee, 40

Carey, 15

Coming To The Mercy Seat

First, GIDEON tosses some "Black Cat Powder" about the place. Then he begins loading his rifle.

GUSSIE LEE appears.

GUSSIE LEE
Gideon, what do you call yourself doing? You look like you're setting a trap for a rat!

GIDEON
He is a rat...a two'legged rat.

GUSSIE LEE
He's our son, and you need to cut this mess out...you didn't even let me finish reading his letter!

GIDEON
I don't wanna hear it! He had a good home and he left. I know why he coming back here 'cause the Obeah woman warned me.

GUSSIE LEE
There you go again with that old superstition mess that nobody believes in except somebody ignorant!

GIDEON
That sweet woman called my friends and my enemies by name and hadn't never laid eyes on me before. How did she know he had hit me up'side the head before he left here? I didn't tell her.

GUSSIE LEE
I don't know how she knew...I just know Carey is not coming

back here to hurt you. He's sick and hurt and he needs us.

GIDEON
That's what he get! He didn't wanna listen to me and go to school.

GUSSIE LEE
Gideon, just let him come long enough for me to see if he's all right.

GIDEON
You better hope he learned some sense, 'cause if he come back here tryin' to run over me, I got a bullet with his name on it.

GUSSIE LEE
Now, you know I'm not gonna stand by and let you hurt my child, Gideon.

GIDEON
Just let him raise his hand to me again! Don't tell me I won't aim and hit him where The Good Lord split him! I should-a killed him that day he told me if he saw me layin' in a ditch bleeding to death, he'd pass on by and let me die.

GUSSIE LEE
He knew it was wrong to talk to you like that, but he's only fifteen, Gideon! He's still a child...speaking like a child, understanding like a child and acting like a child.

GIDEON
He must-a thought he was a man to be bucking up to me...so he better start acting like one. I didn't live under my daddy's roof when I was his age.

Coming To The Mercy Seat

GUSSIE LEE
Your son's been trying to be a man, to prove he could make it on his own. He's not asking to live under this roof. If you knew how to read, you would see that.

GIDEON
I don't need to read to know what I know. Let him stay on out there in whatever den he's in. He probably just got out-a jail.

GUSSIE LEE
He wasn't in jail, no such-a-thing. He's been working on hog farms and in strawberry fields. Some men jumped him and left him naked and half-dead. Thank the Lord, some hoboes nursed him back.

GIDEON
I told him a hard head make a soft behind!

GUSSIE LEE
He was trying to make some money to send home to you.

GIDEON
Aw, git'away from here with that nonsense!

GUSSIE LEE
That's what he says in the letter.

GIDEON
He ain't gotta send me nothing! The time he should-a been bringing me his money, he gave it to that teacher at that school to save for him. It wasn't even enough to keep me in cigars for a week...he just didn't wanna see me with it. I could-a put it away for him. I was his daddy...s'pozed-to-be daddy. He was living under my roof, eatin' my food. Now

he ain't got two nickels to rub together, so he coming back here with a hand'full-a *gimme*. Let him go live with that teacher.

GUSSIE LEE

There's something I been wanting to say to you for a long time, Gideon. All you've been thinking about these past few months is your own hurt. But when the sheep stray, it's the shepherd's fault. If you hadn't been trying to beat your son for that dev'lish money, he wouldn't-a struck out at you. He said he didn't take the money.

GIDEON

He always said he didn't do nothing. And the Bible say *spare the rod and spoil the child.*

GUSSIE LEE

It also says *provoke not your children to wrath.* How many times did I misplace money, only to find it later on right where I laid it?

GIDEON

There you go again! You see what I mean? No matter what I say, you wanna hide him behind your skirt'tail. That's why he turned out the way he did.

GUSSIE LEE

Alright, Gideon, I'm through with it! I'm just gonna leave you to God 'cause I can see your heart just ain't big enough to forgive nobody! You need a heart transplant, that's what! Who ever heard of a father waiting to ambush his own son?

GIDEON

I'm waiting for a dog I raised that bit me, and I ain't gonna get bit twice by the same dog!

Coming To The Mercy Seat

>GUSSIE LEE

I'm waiting for a son who loved his father, before son *and* father started misunderstanding each other.

>GIDEON

He didn't love me after he started going to that school and got a swelled head, giving me word for word. Just 'cause I can't read n' write, it don't make me no fool.

>(In the distance, GUSSIE LEE thinks she sees CAREY.)

>GUSSIE LEE

Who is this coming here? That look like my child! Carey? Oh, Lord, that is him!

>(GIDEON readies his rifle.)

>GUSSIE LEE runs to CAREY, who is unshaven and disheveled)

>CAREY

Mama, I'm all right...I'm all right!

>GUSSIE LEE

My baby! Lord, thank you! Thank you for sending our son back home safe!

>GIDEON

Well, well, well! Look what the cat done drug in!

>CAREY

Hello, daddy.

J.e Franklin

GIDEON
Didn't I tell you if you ever came back here, I was gonna kill you?

CAREY
Yes-sir, daddy...I remember.

GIDEON
You don't believe I'll shoot you, do you?

CAREY
Yes-sir, I believe you'll do it, daddy.

GIDEON
I don't know why you calling me *daddy*...you ain't been no kind-a son to me.

GUSSIE LEE
Gideon, why don't you cut this foolishness out and put that gun down?! If you pull that trigger, you know you gonna have to shoot me, too!

CAREY
Mama, I don't blame him. He's right. I ain't fit to be called his son. I ain't even fit to tell my father I love him, but I'm gonna say it anyway. I love you, daddy.

GUSSIE LEE
See there, Gideon? I told you your son still loves you! How can you turn from him!?

GIDEON
He turned from me! I went to that school to see him that time, and he ran and hid 'cause he was shamed of me.

Coming To The Mercy Seat

CAREY
I know how much I must-a hurt you, daddy, and I was wrong. But it wasn't you I was shamed of...it was me...shamed of being poor and not having nice clothes like other boys...just shamed of myself. I had to hear this from a hobo before I could come to my senses and realize what you were trying to teach me.

GIDEON
See there?! I told you, didn't I?

CAREY
Yes-sir, daddy, you told me. I was hard-headed.

GIDEON
I said that! I told your mama you was hard-headed, but she always wanna 'spute my word!

GUSSIE LEE
Gideon, look at how he's humbling himself!

CAREY
Move, mama. Let me get down on my knees to my father...and if he can't forgive me, he'll never see me again in this life.

GUSSIE LEE
Oh, son, don't talk this way!

CAREY
At first, I wished them hoboes had let me die. Then I asked God to let me live long enough to make it home to ask you to forgive me for hurting you, daddy...

GUSSIE LEE
Bless your heart! Your daddy wants to forgive you! Gideon, give him a sign. Can't you see he's changed.

(CAREY falls humbly to his knees.)

GIDEON
How come you stayed all this time without writing your mama? You know she was worried about you.

CAREY
I started a lot-a letters, but I wanted to mail *me* in 'em. I wanted to come back sooner, but I was scared you wouldn't forgive me, and even more scared you still believe I lied to you about taking that money, and I didn't lie, daddy. I told you the truth. All these months, I kept saying, "If only my father would believe me." Now it's all right if you don't believe me...I just want you to forgive me for hitting you, because if you don't, I know I'll never be a man.

GUSSIE LEE
Your daddy's good-hearted deep down in him...he's just set in his ways.

GIDEON
Sometime I had asked myself was I right or wrong.

CAREY
I know I was wrong for raising my hand to you.

GIDEON
What hurt'ed me more than that stick, I put my X on your report card, and I saw where you had spit'ed on the pencil and rubbed it off.

Coming To The Mercy Seat

GUSSIE LEE
He didn't know no better, Gideon!

CAREY
Yes, I did, mama. You and daddy taught me right from wrong, and I'm old enough to know better. I saw that cardboard in the bottom of my father's shoes...who did I think he was sacrificing for? I wasn't thinking about nobody but myself, and I wish them hoboes had let me die!

GUSSIE LEE
Hush, now! I don't wanna hear that kind-a talk!

(GIDEON tosses down the rifle.)

CAREY
I'm leaving now, mama...I got my sign.

GUSSIE LEE
Leaving? Leaving for where?! You just got here. Carey, don't do this! You wanna kill your poor mama with that kind-a talk?

CAREY
Mama, let me go... I got my sign...I wanna go. Let me go.

GUSSIE LEE
Gideon, don't let him do this! Don't y'all know what this does to a mother's heart?!

GIDEON
I ain't said he had to go nowhere...he know he ain't ate nothing.

CAREY
I'm full now, daddy. I have what I came for. I have to go now...I wanna go.

GUSSIE LEE
Carey, don't do this! Lord'have'mercy! Don't just run off again like this!

CAREY
I promise I'll write to you this time, and let you know where I am...I promise! I just wanna put my arms around my father before I go, though I know I don't deserve it.

GUSSIE LEE
Gideon, let him put his arms around you! Bless his heart!

(GIDEON, struggling with his emotions, hesitates. Finally, he allows his son to embrace him. GUSSIE LEE stands aside and weeps.)

CAREY
My father...my father!

END

Coming To The Mercy Seat

Can't tell you what it's like to not have one
The hugs and kisses,
Encouragement and strength
Sacrifices they make, going to all lengths...

To make sure you have
What they never had
Loving you as only a mother could

If I had my way....
Well, this ain't about me...
It's about Solomon's Way

N'zinga

SOLOMON'S WAY

CHARACTERS IN ORDER OF APPEARANCE

EMILE, 60 plus

ANNA, 60 plus

THE MOTHER, 75 plus

EMILE is onstage, visibly agitated.

ANNA enters.

ANNA
Emile, won't you at least come and meet her?

EMILE
Anna, why can't you tend to your business sometimes and leave well-enough alone?

ANNA
I thought you'd be happy to see her.

EMILE
What made you think I wasn't already happy?

ANNA
I'm not blind, Emile. I know a broke heart when I see one.

EMILE
If it *is* broke, she ain't the one can fix it!

ANNA
Well, somebody better fix something around here, 'cause you ain't been so pleasant to live with every since you found them dev'lish papers.

EMILE
Don't think I ain't cursed the day I found 'em!

ANNA
Why did you let me write all them letters and run the phone bill up, calling every agency in this land year after year after

Coming To The Mercy Seat

year...?

EMILE
Who told you to do all that? Did I tell you to look for any people of mine?

ANNA
You didn't try to stop me! You knew the aggravation I was going through to make them people listen and understand...!

EMILE
You didn't see *me* looking!

ANNA
I saw you studying every face on every old person you saw, trying to see some resemblance. Folks must-a thought we was both crazy, staring at 'em like that!

EMILE
I thought you was looking for your own people.

ANNA
You ain't thought no such-a thing. Yes, I was looking for my people. I'm still hoping and praying I'll find 'em, just like I found yours. But both of us would be pointing and saying, "Look, Emile, you feature that man over there!" And every now and then you'd tell me, "Look, Anna, that lady over there look just like you! Don't you think you feature her?!"

EMILE
I ain't got nothing to say to that lady, Anna. If she ain't dead, she can't tell me nothing!

(A beat.)

ANNA
Emile, when we were in foster care together, we made a pact. We said whoever found their parents first, they would be both our parents. If I found mine first, I'd beg 'em to adopt you...if you found yours first...

EMILE
Anna, we ain't no foster kids no more! We grown! We don't need no parents now!

ANNA
I know, Emile!

EMILE
You don't act like you know it! What you want me to do, drag that woman into court and tell the judge we wanna be adopted? People our age don't get adopted!

ANNA
Stop playing with me! You know I don't like that!

EMILE
Then don't provoke me!

ANNA
All right! Just take it easy!

EMILE
You the one better take it easy!

ANNA
Emile...neither one of us didn't have no kind-a childhood worth talking about. Both of us got teased and laughed at for not having no parents...

Coming To The Mercy Seat

EMILE
I kicked plenty ass about it, too!

ANNA
I took that stuff to heart, and maybe you took it harder than I did...I don't know. It still hurt when I think about it. I would go to a friend's house after school, and they would be saying, "Mother, can I walk to school tomorrow," and "Mother, can I wear my new dress tomorrow?" I know what age I am, but I still feel like a little child in my heart. I can't help this longing that won't go away. I don't wanna leave this world knowing I was passed from hand to hand and never belonged to nobody. You have to know how much this hurts me, to never call no woman *mother*! That's my mother-in-law in there! When God joined you and me together, that made us one body with whoever is your kin. It's like she's my kin and my mother, too, Emile. Maybe that's the closest I'll get to a mother. Don't take this from me.

EMILE
Anna, I thought she was dead!

ANNA
Well, now you know she ain't dead. You can't just keep her in there waiting...you gotta give her some kind-a sign.

EMILE
Give her a sign! What sign did I get from her all these years?

ANNA
Emile, she said she looked for you...

EMILE
Looked for me! What else can she say?

ANNA
The records were sealed! You know what it's like when the state don't want you to know something.

EMILE
For all I know, she could-a been off somewhere living the life of Reiley! I found out she had other children, and she kept them. She didn't give them away. I know why she looked me up...'cause she done got old and feeble and want somebody to take care of her. Why don't she go ask the ones she kept?

ANNA
I don't know. Give your mother a chance to explain why she...

EMILE
Woah, woah, woah...stop this right now! Don't be calling her my *mother*. She might-a been the one brought me into this world, but who fed me and looked after me? I already buried the only mom and pop I ever knew.

ANNA
The ones you said used to beat you and punish you, and make you sleep up on the roof in the cold? The ones who burned up some of the papers so you wouldn't even find out what your real name was?

(A beat.)

EMILE
You ain't got no right to bring that up.

ANNA
I didn't do it to hurt you, Emile...I was just...

Coming To The Mercy Seat

EMILE
We had some good times and we had some bad times.

ANNA
I'm sure your mother was praying for you during them bad time.

EMILE
Nevermind the prayers! Where was she *at* during them bad times?

ANNA
Emile, she wants to answer all your questions.

EMILE
You think I owe her something, don't you? 'Cause I know how you think...!

ANNA
Not *owe*! I know better than to use that word with you...but I do think it's time for you to forgive and forget, Emile.

EMILE
Don't tell me when it's time for me to do something! I'm the only one that's got a right to say when it's time for me to do something! Let God do the forgiving! I don't forgive and I don't forget!

ANNA
I know. But if my mother walked through that door right now, I wouldn't care about why or what...

EMILE
That's you, that ain't me. The woman ain't even wanted me

just throwed me away...!

ANNA

Emile...you're a good man...but sometime you hurt people!

EMILE

I ain't did nothing to her! What did I do to her?! Hey, where's King Solomon at? Go get Solomon! Tell him to bring his sword and go'on cut me in-two! You get half and she get half! Would that satisfy you! All my life I ain't been nothing but a piece-a man, nohow...!

ANNA

Cut it out! Just cut it out, Emile!

(A beat.)

EMILE

I already called one woman *mother*. Now, I'm through with it! How'm I gonna have two mothers? ...'less I be born twice!

ANNA

What do we know about the mysteries of life? I know people born with a veil who say they've lived before. Sometimes I feel I've been here before. When we're born, do we get issued a ration book: one parent for you, two for somebody else, none for me? Does God lay our lives out for us? I don't know. I told your mother she'd be proud of the man you turned out to be.

EMILE

No thanks to her!

Coming To The Mercy Seat

ANNA
Who should get thanked for what we become? Pastor said, "Even when someone hurts us, we're graced! If that hurt can help us feel what others go through, we're graced!" Don't think for a minute that I don't feel what you're going through now. I've been wanting to tell you something. I never told before now 'cause I've been scared you'd cut me to the quick with it whenever you got angry with me...and you still might.

EMILE
What?

ANNA
While I was looking for your people, I found out that my mother wrapped me in a bloody towel and left me in a garbage can!

EMILE
Anna! A garbage can...?

ANNA
...if a homeless man hadn't been looking for something to eat, I wouldn't be here now...graced and feeling your pain!

EMILE
That wench left you to die!

ANNA
I don't want you to judge her, Emile!

EMILE
Don't you hate her?!

ANNA
One mind does. One mind hates her so, I feel paralyzed! But one mind says, *"Anna, you know what it is for a young girl to be scared and alone in this world."*

EMILE
Don't be scared-a me throwing that in your face. I hope God strike me dead if ever I do that!

ANNA
I don't think I could take it.

EMILE
You trust me more than I trust myself! I hear the devil telling me to call that woman all the curse words I used when I would get drunk and crazy. I know if I stoop that low, I'll shorten my days on this earth. I ain't got many left, nohow! I just want her to go'on back where she came from. I don't even wanna know why she dumped me and kept the others.

ANNA
Dumped? No, Emile, you weren't dumped! Your mother had you baptized!

EMILE
Baptized? She told you that?

ANNA
I saw your baptizing papers! She's got them inside a old Bible she must've had for years! And she showed me your baby pictures! I wish somebody had baby pictures of me!

EMILE
Do she have pictures of my father?

Coming To The Mercy Seat

ANNA
I'm sure she does...I'll go ask her...

(ANNA makes a start.)

EMILE
Wait, will ya'? Ha'mercy, Anna! I say two words and off you wanna fly...!

ANNA
She's been sitting in there all this time with everything in her lap.

EMILE
Well, just hold your horses!

ANNA
All right, Emile. I won't move till you tell me to move.

EMILE
I-God, woman! Gimme a chance here! I had this picture all painted... now y'awl done come along and painted all over it! It was supposed to be her *and* my father. They was supposed to come to the door...or the phone would ring...or a letter would come. After a while, I just figured they'd turned their backs on me forever, and I didn't even wanna see 'em no more!

ANNA
Your mother told me, if you come in there and ask her to leave, she'll go.

EMILE
I don't wanna go in there.

ANNA
Can she come in here?

EMILE
If she want to.

(ANNA hugs EMILE, then leaves the room.)

(After a few seconds, MOTHER appears, clutching a Bible. ANNA stands apart, hopeful.)

ANNA
Mother...this is your son, Emile.

(EMILE keeps his back turned.)

MOTHER
Emile...ain't you gonna speak to your mother?

ANNA
He's gonna speak to you, mother...!

MOTHER
I been praying for this day all my life!

(EMILE does not acknowledge her.)

ANNA
Emile, this is your mother...

MOTHER
Son, there wasn't a day went by that I wasn't on my knees asking God to let me see you one mo' time before I closed my

Coming To The Mercy Seat

eyes, and praise God, my prayers have been answered! I just wanted to live long enough to tell you I always loved you. I never gave you away, honey. I was just a young girl. Me and your daddy was at a church camp. While we were there, I became pregnant with you, but our parents wouldn't let us marry. After you was born, I had you baptized, and I kept you and fed you and dressed you proper. But back then; they wouldn't let young girls have families. And one day, my uncle lured me away from the house. Somebody came and got you while I was gone. They had it all planned. Nobody would tell me or your daddy where they'd took you. When we got old enough, we ran away and married. We asked around and looked and looked for you. All these years! That's what kilt your daddy! I promised him 'fore he died as long as I had breath in my body, I'd never stop looking for you, honey! And thank the Lord, I done found you! Praise God! Praise God!

      (EMILE faces his mother and the two embrace tearfully.)

      ANNA
Mother, your son has suffered so much! He's suffered so much!
      MOTHER
Lord, Lord, Lord! Lord, Lord, Lord!

      (ANNA stands aside, weeping.)

<u>END</u>

Playwright J.e Franklin and Director Tisch Jones on the set of UNI's Bertha Martin Theater production of Grey Panthers: Coming To The Mercy Seat.

(Photo by Photographer on assignment from The Waterloo Cedar Falls Courier)

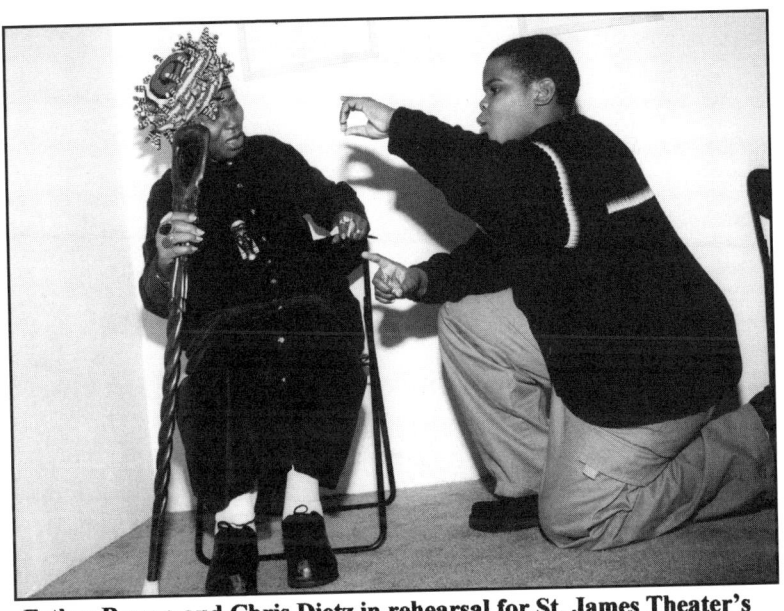
Esther Brown and Chris Dietz in rehearsal for St. James Theater's Production of The Final Passion of St. Martin The King.

Photo By Kwame Brathwaite

Director Eric Coleman at St. James Theatre, rehearsing production of Shacking Up Grey

Photo By Jerry Komia Domatob

Actress Maggie Henderson in production of Puttin' Mamma In The Ground

Photo By Marissa Henderson

Other Works by J. e Franklin

Blackbird
Black Girl
Christchild
Little Jo
Miss Honey's Young'uns
Miss N'Victus
The Gift
The Onliest One That Can't Go Nowhere
The Prodigal Sister
Whistling Girls and Crowing Hens
Wonderchild

All plays available for production and purchase
Contact us via email at **JE413@AOL.COM**

Other Products By

SunRASon Production Company

Mental Eye-roglyphics (Book)
By Tehut-Nine

A Hip Hop Story (Book)
By Heru Ptah

Mind Magician (CD)
By Tehut-Nine

All items above available online at

www.sunrason.com

About the Author

Ms. J. e Franklin

J. e Franklin is the founder and producing artistic director of Blackgirl Ensemble Theater, Inc., located in the historic Sugar Hill district of Harlem. She attended The University of Texas in Austin, and Union Theological Seminary in New York. Her non-fiction book BLACK GIRL: From Genesis to Revelations, is an autobiographical account of the development of her first major work from television to stage and screen. In 1984, The McGinn-Cazale Second Stage Theater in New York City produced BLACK GIRL as part of its series on American Classics.

In addition to BLACK GIRL, Ms. Franklin's other professional productions include CHRISTCHILD, THE PRODIGAL SISTER, UNDER HEAVEN'S EYE 'TIL COCKCROW, THE ONLIEST ONE WHO CAN'T GO NOWHERE, and her signature body of work: five decatets of Ten-Minute folk dramas, including GREY PANTHERS: Coming to the Mercy Seat, and PRECIOUS MEMORIES: The Black History Series. Ms. Franklin's works have been performed at theaters around the world, including, the Kwa Muhle Theater in South Africa, the Instituto de Las Culturo in Mexico, and the world-famous Apollo Theater in Harlem.

Her works have appeared in major anthologies, including WOMEN PLAYWRIGHTS: The Best Plays of 1993, published by Smith & Kraus, 1994; BLACK DRAMA IN AMERICA, Second Edition, published by Howard University Press, 1994; THE BEST AMERICAN SHORT PLAYS OF 1994-95, published by Applause Theater Books, 1996; STURDY BLACK BRIDGES ON THE AMERICAN STAGE, published by Aachen University Press, Aachen,

Germany, 1997; and in the Seventh Edition of PERRINE'S LITERATURE: STRUCTURE, SOUND AND SENSE, Published by Harcourt-Brace, 1997.

Her awards include a Rockefeller Fellowship, a New York Drama Desk Award, and fellowships from The New York Foundation for the Arts and The National Endowment for the Arts. She is a fellow of the U. S./MEXICO Artists Exchange Program, a Eugene O'Neill fellow, a winner of The John F. Kennedy Center's New American Play Award for her play CHRISTCHILD, and, most recently, the recipient of a Proclamation from the City Council for her outstanding contributions to the cultural life of New York City.

Ms. Franklin has been resident playwright at Rites & Reason Theater of Brown University, and visiting assistant professor in the Department of Theater Arts at The University of Iowa. One of Ms. Franklin's current projects includes "The Sanctuary Series," a body of Ten-Minute plays suitable for performance during worship services and now being performed at churches throughout the country.

Ms. Franklin is the director of drama ministry at St. James Presbyterian Church in Harlem, and an adjunct professor in the Department of Languages and Literature at Touro College.

Coming Soon

Precious Memories: The Black History Series
The 2nd Decatet

By J.e Franklin

The plays in this series explore the American culture through the lives and experiences of African-American historical personalities who boldly confronted the political forces of their day, and who left us the benefit of their wisdom in overcoming these forces.

Drawing on the voice, rhythm and value system of the African-American cultural tradition, the plays are primarily inter-generational, but the stories are experienced through an elder-centered vision, creating a compressed sense of period and content which helps audiences understand history in compelling ways that will renew their spirit and sense of courage.

The plays have been written and developed specifically for presentation in intimate spaces, which need no set or elaborate technical requirements. The Company has performed in libraries, churches, community centers, hospitals, prisons, schools, colleges and universities, and at conferences on four continents. The plays are age-appropriate and language-appropriate for all audiences.

DEM BONES, DEM DRY BONES

How important are our ancestors, and what do we owe them? When a construction crew accidentally unearths the remains of a turn-of-the century African Burial Ground in lower Manhattan, a young street hustler sees this as an opportunity for commerce. He fills his sacks with the precious rocks and dirt from the burial site and sets up his vending table. But a feisty, down-on-her-luck former socialite, a self-appointed protector of the site, conjures up the spirit of the ancestors and turns the hustler's mind inside-out.

A DEATH IN MEMPHIS

How deeply did the death of Dr. Martin Luther King, Jr. impact on our lives? In this play, fourteen-year-old Isaac strays away from his schoolmates during a class trip to Memphis, Tennessee. Hoping to get a rare interview with Dr. Martin Luther King, Jr. and return to school as the star of his class, he wanders near the Lorraine Motel. But before Isaac can get the opportunity to meet Dr. King, his hero is cut down by an assassin's bullet. Who will tell him about his hero now?

ISHMAEL'S BOOKER-T PROJECT

Does the life of Booker T. Washington hold any value for today's youth? In this play, fifteen year old Ishmael stops attending school after a series of embarrassing failures and mishaps. A former history teacher visits him at his home and persuades him to work on a field project which includes Booker T-Washington's autobiography _Up From Slavery_. Ishmael meets grumpy but good-hearted Pop Lewis, a community elder who reluctantly mentors him, shepherds him through his pain, and helps him find his courage.

THAT BAILEY BOY

How important was reading to enslaved Africans? This bio-play, written in rhymed couplets, introduces audiences to ten-year-old Frederick Douglass, experiencing the stings of racial hatred after the mistress of the plantation is forbidden to teach him to read. But the experience helps Frederick understand that reading is the key to obtaining his freedom. With the help of Aunt Rachel, an elder who has taken the boy to her heart, Frederick plots his escape and goes on to become an international spokesman for his people.

TAKE THE CASE OF SAMPSON

How do new styles and fads affect the economies of struggling communities? In this play, a national celebrity is coming to town with a hairstyle, which threatens the only lucrative business in the community. When the sorority, which invited the celebrity, fails to find a way to un-invite her, they persuade the local beauty shop to picket and boycott the affair. But the scheme backfires when a respected community elder confronts the conspirators.

THE NAME GAME

What's in a name? What should African-Americans call themselves? Colored, Negro, Black, African-American, or just plain American? This question has been debated throughout America's racial history. In this play, based on historical fact, delegates meet at one of the mass meetings which were organized in principal cities around the country to carry out an injunction with respect to the name. Heated opinions inflame tempers, but the wiser voices prevail.

PAYBACK! I'M MAD!
Does *reparations* mean to repay or to repair? This bio-play introduces audiences to the late Queen Mother Moore. In this play, she is leading a demonstration in front of a prestigious church, when a young member of The Association of Guardians (a Black fraternal organization within the police department) is sent to arrest her. The young officer, caught on the horns of a dilemma, echoes the Shakespearean question, must I serve my master, or must I serve my people?

THAT'S WHY THEY CALLS US COLORED, BLESS THEIR HEARTS
Does the word *race* have the same meaning as the word *color*? Are our *racial* identities fixed, or is *race* a fluid concept? In this play, a descendant of a slave-holding Dutchman searches among tombstones and through genealogical records to learn of his ancestral roots. While surfing the internet, he finds someone who is wearing his unusual surname and gets invited to a family reunion. Bringing with him a cherished family photo of his great-grand-father, he arrives at the reunion to find the whole room filled with Black people and realizes that, not only is he African-American, but that the bloodline of slaves runs through his veins.

THE OLD ROMAN
What should an oppressed people feel about the symbols of their oppressors? This bio-play introduces audiences to Bishop Henry McNeal Turner. Embittered by his experiences as a chaplain in the United States Army during the Civil War and post-Civil War era, the bishop splits his congregation down the middle on the question of the American flag. After his death, congregants ask, " Should the flag be draped over the bishop's coffin, or can a flag-draped coffin be a deterrent to the white terrorists who plague the Black community?"

MOTHER KING

What is it like being the daughter of a minister, the wife of a minister, and the mother of two ministers? This bio-play introduces audiences to the mother of the late Rev. Dr. Martin Luther King, Jr. A few days after the assassination of her son, Mother King tries to recover her son's memory. What she recovers instead are memories of her own aborted youth and ambitions. The play paints a portrait of the limitations and suppressed dreams of a young girl growing up in the church.

NOTES